D1604661

Famous Flyers

Claire Chennault
Amelia Earhart
Charles Lindbergh
Eddie Rickenbacker
Manfred von Richthofen
Chuck Yeager

Manfred von Richthofen

Earle Rice Jr.

CHELSEA HOUSE
PUBLISHERS
A Haights Cross Communications Company

Philadelphia

Frontis: Manfred von Richthofen, "the Red Baron," poses in his German officer's uniform in this portrait taken at the beginning of World War I.

CHELSEA HOUSE PUBLISHERS

VP, NEW PRODUCT DEVELOPMENT Sally Cheney
DIRECTOR OF PRODUCTION Kim Shinners
CREATIVE MANAGER Takeshi Takahashi
MANUFACTURING MANAGER Diann Grasse

Staff for MANFRED VON RICHTHOFEN

EXECUTIVE EDITOR Lee Marcott
ASSOCIATE EDITOR Bill Conn
PRODUCTION EDITOR Jaimie Winkler
PICTURE RESEARCHER Sarah Bloom
SERIES DESIGNER Keith Trego
COVER DESIGNER Keith Trego
LAYOUT 21st Century Publishing and Communications, Inc.

A Haights Cross Communications ✈ Company

http://www.chelseahouse.com

First Printing

1 3 5 7 9 8 6 4 2

Library of Congress Cataloging-in-Publication Data applied for.

ISBN 0-7910-7214-2

CONTENTS

Spinning
Out of Control

O n July 6, 1917, the morning was bright and clear at Marcke, on the southwest edge of Courtrai, Belgium. In the adjacent area named Marckebeke—a sprawling expanse of green lawns quartering a castle and lesser buildings—the estate of Baron Jean de Bethune was undergoing conversion for military use. Its proximity to the Western Front provided an ideal location from which the Imperial German Air Service could conduct the business of war. It had recently become the home of *Jagdgeschwader 1* (Fighter Wing 1), commanded by Germany's ace of aces, Manfred *Freiherr* (Baron) von Richthofen.

Crown Prince Rupprecht of Bavaria, a nominal commander on the Western Front, had announced the formation of Jagdgeschwader 1 (JG 1) 12 days earlier on June 24, 1917. Richthofen, whose aerial victories now totaled 57, had just returned from leave to take command of the new fighter wing. On that perfect July morning, Richthofen had decided to personally lead one of his new fighter wing's *Jastas* (a contraction of *Jagdstaffel*, which means "hunting section" in German) on a mission to repel low-flying enemy trench-strafers. (Functionally, a Jasta closely resembled an Allied—chiefly, a British, French, or American—fighter squadron.)

Of the fighter wing's four Jastas, numbered 4, 6, 10, and 11,

The Albatros fighter planes that formed the core of the Jastas commanded by Baron von Richthofen would become known as the "Flying Circus" for their gaudy colors and their pilots' ability to maneuver quickly from airfield to airfield.

Richthofen's rotating duty schedule called for Jasta 11 to fly the mission. Before climbing into his all-red Albatros D.V fighter plane, the man who called himself "the red air fighter" (*Der Rote Kampfflieger*) paused briefly to survey the bright summer sky and the pastoral beauty of his surroundings. It was a perfect day for the hunt. And Germany knew no better hunter.

Richthofen took off with his Jasta 11 subordinates, his Albatros leading the way, at 1030 (military time uses a twenty-four-hour clock, with noon set as 1200 hours, 1:00 P.M. as 1300, and so on to midnight, set as 2400 hours). Because he painted his personal aircraft red in defiance of both his adversaries and the odds of surviving combat over the Western Front, Richthofen had quickly gained fame as "the Red Baron." He led his pilots to a height of 4,000 meters (13,124 feet), leveled off, and set a westerly course for the front.

Meanwhile, at 0950 hours, six lumbering, two-seat F.E.2d pusher biplanes had lifted off the British airfield at Ste.-Marie-Cappel in northern France, just south of Cassel, midway between St.-Omer and Bailleul. The F.E.2s belonged to 20 Squadron of the Royal Flying Corps (RFC) and were led by Captain Donald Charles Cunnell, Hampshire Regiment/RFC. Their mission that morning was to fly an offensive patrol (OP) over the central Western Front. "[I]n other words," as Second Lieutenant Albert Edward Woodbridge, Cunnell's observer, recalled a few years later, "we were supposed to go out and light into any enemy planes we could find."

Because the German Albatros and Halberstadt fighters "could fly rings around us and shoot hell out of us from that blind spot under our tails," Woodbridge went on, "we were like butterflies sent out to insult eagles."

The F.E.2, manufactured by the Royal Aircraft Factory (later called the Royal Aircraft Establishment so as not to be confused with the Royal Air Force after April 1, 1918), was called a pusher-type aircraft because its 250-horsepower (hp) Rolls-Royce engine was mounted behind the pilot. The observer sat forward of the pilot in a kind of gondola with

 ## The Albatros Fighters

Nearly 5,000 Albatros fighter planes of varying models were produced by the German government during World War I, making the Albatros one of the most readily recognizable and popular aircraft of the war. Many German flying aces (a pilot with 5 or more confirmed kills) scored the majority of their victories in an Albatros. Manfred von Richthofen himself scored 49 of his 80 victories in Albatros fighters.

Perhaps the most infamous plane flown by Richthofen was the Albatros D.III, which he used to deadly effect against the Allies in 1917 during the month that came to be known as "Bloody April." In a move that taunted his enemies and inspired his fellow pilots, Richthofen painted his Albatros bright red—earning himself the legendary nickname, "the Red Baron."

The bark of Richthofen's all-red Albatros D.III was supported by the bite of Germany's latest aeronautical design. Although not significantly faster or more maneuverable, the D.III did have one distinct advantage when compared to its predecessors: increased visibility.

Albatros chief designer Robert Thelen studied the French Nieuport Scout before redesigning the D.II. He adopted a design similar to the Nieuport's sesquiplane layout, which called for a lower wing with a smaller width than the upper wing. Because of the decreased width, the lower wing only needed a single main spar (the longitudinal member that holds the ribs of the wing) and allowed the designer to adopt a V strut (the structure between top and bottom wings), which increased the pilot's field of vision.

Although the lower wing occasionally failed during difficult maneuvers—a fact Richthofen would discover firsthand—the Albatros D.III was widely accepted by German aviators. The Red Baron shot down 21 Allied aircraft during Bloody April using the Albatros D.III.

SPAN: 29 feet, 8 inches. LENGTH: 24 feet. ENGINE: 175 hp Mercedes D.IIIa six-cylinder. ARMAMENT: two synchronized 7.92-mm Spandau machine guns. MAXIMUM SPEED: 109 mph at 3,281 feet. SERVICE CEILING: 18,000 feet wheels that was attached to the wings by wooden spars and to the tail section by an open, three-plane wooden trellis that formed an inverted pyramid.

The ungainly looking aircraft was armed with three Lewis machine guns—one each mounted on pivots to the front and rear of the observer's cockpit and fired by him, and a third fixed to the right side of the forward cockpit and fired by a trigger on the pilot's controls. The F.E.2 stood less than an even chance against the concentrated fire of the Albatros's twin Spandau machine guns that were affixed to the top of the fuselage in front of the pilot and synchronized to fire through the propeller.

Against the more advanced German fighters, the life expectancy of F.E.2 crews over the Western Front was often measured in days. As Woodbridge put it, "We were 'cold meat,' and most of us knew it." But ordered to engage the enemy, the RFC airmen had no choice except to "carry on." That day, however, a favorable east wind whistled through the spars and support wires of their awkward machines as they droned along toward their assigned patrol area over Comines, Warneton, and Freilinghein. Perhaps the friendly east wind augured well for whatever lay ahead for the Englishmen. (In western Europe, the prevailing winds generally blow from west to east. Thus they would usually carry Allied aircraft eastward and force Allied airmen to fight over enemy territory most of the time. German pilots only rarely had to contend with unfavorable winds that would reverse their circumstances and drive them westward to battle over hostile terrain. For the Germans, east winds were ill winds that blew no good.) And so it was for the Red Baron and his Jasta 11 pilots that morning when they met their counterparts of the RFC's 20 Squadron in the clear skies over Comines-Warneton.

The F.E.s (called "Fees") usually carried a few twenty-pound bombs to drop on targets of opportunity. This morning was no exception. Captain Cunnell led his squadron mates to a favorite target area at Houthem, alongside the Ypres-Comines Canal, and they dropped their bombs. Shortly after Cunnell and his mates turned back from the northern-most point of their patrol, they sighted a large formation of enemy fighters. The enemy aircraft—about 40 Albatros Scouts in groups that numbered between eight and twenty—had positioned themselves between the British lines and Cunnell's machines.

"My word," Lieutenant Woodbridge declared later, "I never saw so many Huns in the air at one time in my life before." ("Hun" is disparaging slang for a German soldier.) Woodbridge went on to describe the ensuing battle:

> Two of them came at us head on, and I think the first one was Richthofen. I recall there wasn't a thing on that machine that wasn't red, and God, how he could fly! I opened fire with the front Lewis, and so did Cunnell with the [fixed] side gun.

The two machines raced at each other at an estimated combined speed of 250 miles an hour. Neither machine wavered. Both held to a collision course. Woodbridge continued:

> Thank God, my Lewis didn't jam. I kept a steady stream of lead pouring into the nose of that machine. He was firing also. I could see my tracers [phosphorus-filled ammunition that leaves a smoky, illuminated trail] splashing along the barrels of his Spandaus and I knew the pilot was sitting right behind them. His lead came whistling past my head and ripping holes in the bathtub [gondola].

A collision seemed certain. But suddenly, with the two machines no more than twenty yards apart, the nose of the all-red Albatros dipped down abruptly and zipped under

The spectacular dogfights—aerial battles fought at close quarters—over the Western Front were the Red Baron's specialty. He was able to take the Albatros D.V through maneuvers that dazzled and defeated his enemies.

Cunnell's F.E.2. Cunnell banked and turned, and he and Woodbridge watched the red Albatros slip into a spin. "It turned over and over and round and round," Woodbridge recollected. "It was no manoeuvre."

The Red Baron's Albatros was spinning out of control. And the ground below was coming up fast to meet Germany's leading air fighter.

Passport to
the Clouds

More than a century after his birth, Manfred Freiherr von Richthofen remains the most famous fighter pilot not only of his own time, but of all time. He was a born hunter and, as many have said, a born killer. Manfred was also a natural leader, revered by his subordinates, esteemed by his superiors, and respected by his foes. His short-cropped blond hair, piercing blue eyes, and medium height and build validated his national image as a modern-day Teutonic knight.

The story of Germany's Red Knight of the Air begins in Breslau, in the (then) Silesia region of Germany (now Wroclaw, Poland), on May 2, 1892. It ends above the Western Front on April 21, 1918, eleven days before his twenty-sixth birthday. But his legend refuses to die.

Born into a family of middle-rank Prussian aristocrats, the young baron spent a brief boyhood developing his hunting and killing skills in the protected game forests of Silesia. In addition to Manfred, two of his siblings were born in Breslau—his older sister Elisabeth on August 8, 1890, and his younger brother Lothar on September 27, 1894. His youngest brother Karl came along on April 16, 1903, after the family

The combination of Manfred's dashing appearance, ability to lead, and killer instinct elicited admiration from his subordinates, superiors, and enemies alike, and served as the foundation for his undying legend.

had moved to their country estate in nearby Schweidnitz (now Swidnica, Poland). "There has scarcely been a von Richthofen without a landed estate," Manfred pointed out in his brief autobiography.

The Richthofens trace their family origins to the mid-16th century in Bernau, near Berlin. Johann Praetorius (1611–1664), a paternal ancestor, migrated to Silesia in the next century. Holy Roman Emperor Leopold I elevated him into the hereditary Bohemian Knighthood under the name of Johann Praetorius von Richthofen (Richt-Hofen, meaning "court of judgment," is a Germanization of Praetorius, a name that is itself rooted in an ancestral Protestant judge's Latinization of his family name from Schultze). Current members of the Richthofen family all descend from Johann Praetorius von Richthofen.

Despite favors rendered unto them by the Holy Roman Empire, the Richthofens remained faithful to their Protestant roots. During the reign of King Friedrich II of Prussia (Frederick the Great), the family supported him in seizing Silesia from the Habsburg dynasty, which had succeeded the Holy Roman Empire in Austria. To reward them, the Prussian monarch elevated the Richthofens to the baronial ranks on November 6, 1741. Richthofen males would henceforth bear the hereditary title of *Freiherr* (baron); their spouses would use the title *Freifrau* (baroness).

Although Manfred's father, Albrecht Freiherr von Richthofen, served as a major in the First Regiment of Cuirassiers, the Richthofen lineage did not evidence a military tradition. (Cuirassiers were mounted soldiers who wore a cuirass, a piece of armor that covered the body from neck to waist.) His father, according to Manfred, was "practically the first member of our branch of the family who had the idea of becoming a professional soldier." A hearing difficulty brought on by an ear infection contracted while saving one of his men from drowning forced Albrecht's early retirement to his villa in Schweidnitz.

At Schweidnitz, Albrecht encouraged his sons to engage in horsemanship and athletics. Manfred most enjoyed swimming and shooting. The forests of the Weistritz (Bystrzyca) Valley offered abundant game, and Manfred learned to double his pleasure by coupling his riding and shooting skills. In childhood, he discovered the thrill of the chase and the adrenaline rush of bagging game from the back of his horse—emotions that he would later experience again and again in the air.

The walls of the Schweidnitz home, adorned with more than 400 mounted deer heads and stuffed birds, attested to Albrecht's own proficiency as a huntsman. His array of trophies also offers evidence of the spaciousness of the Richthofen living quarters. Young Manfred would soon acquire the same hunter's compulsion to collect and display symbols of his conquests.

Manfred's first trophy, as his mother liked to recall, was a small piece of brown pasteboard with three duck feathers affixed to it with sealing wax. Kunigunde Freifrau von Richthofen explained the story behind her son's "prize" this way:

> We passed our vacations in the country with Grandmother. One day Manfred could not suppress his fast-developing passion for hunting. He had his first air rifle and with it killed three or four of Grandmother's tame ducks that he found swimming in a little pond near the house. He proudly related his exploit to his grandmother, and I started to reprimand him. His good old grandmother stopped me from scolding him because, as she said, he had been right in confessing his misdeed.

Hunting and riding also served as the main hobbies of family members on the young baron's maternal side. His mother belonged to the von Schickfuss und Neudorff family, and her brother, Alexander, became well known for his hunting prowess. After bagging untold varieties of horned and feathered wildlife in the forests of Silesia, Alexander broadened his quest for new kinds of quarry in the wilds of Africa, in Ceylon, and in Hungary. Manfred drew inspiration for his own love of the hunt from the colorful tales of Uncle Alexander, a frequent visitor in the Richthofen household.

In watching his eldest son develop, Albrecht no doubt saw in him the makings of a fine Prussian officer. Manfred's noble bloodline, his superb horsemanship and natural athletic ability, and his equally inbred leadership qualities combined the essential characteristics required for a successful career in the cavalry. Albrecht perhaps perceived Manfred as an extension of himself—a son capable of rising to the summit of the military profession and achieving the goal that had eluded the father.

In Manfred's generation, a half-dozen of his cousins would serve and perish in the cavalry in the coming war. His great-uncle, godfather, and namesake became another role model for the young baron. "I have been named after my uncle Manfred who, in peacetime, was Adjutant to His Majesty [Kaiser Wilhelm II] and Commander of the Corps of the Guards," Manfred wrote later. "During the war he has been Commander of a Corps of Cavalry."

In 1903, to prepare young Manfred for a similar career path, Albrecht enrolled him as a cadet in the military school at Wahlstatt (Legnickie Pole) at the age of eleven. "I was not particularly eager to become a Cadet," Manfred admitted later, "but my father wished it. So my wishes were not consulted." Young Prussians did not question the will of their fathers. Manfred did not care much for either the discipline or the curriculum at Wahlstatt and did just enough to pass. But he enjoyed sports and excelled in gymnastics.

Although slight of build in his youth, Manfred was wiry

As a young boy embarking on a military career, Manfred had little cause to imagine that he would someday be honored by Germany's supreme ruler, Kaiser Wilhelm II (pictured here), for his heroics as a flying ace.

and agile. During his cadet years, his physical ability and the way he carried himself—his bearing—spared him the sorts of harassment and abuse that older boys often heap upon those who appear weaker than themselves. At Wahlstatt, Manfred learned to follow orders, to work within a military establishment at all levels, and to command the recognition and respect of his peers. It was a hard life, but that is how soldiers are made. And after six years at Wahlstatt, and another two years at the prestigious Royal Prussian Military Academy at Gross-Lichterfelde, near Potsdam, Manfred emerged in 1911 at the age of nineteen as a soldier of the first order.

Upon graduation, the academy posted Manfred as a *Fahnenjunker* (officer candidate) to the First Uhlan Regiment Kaiser Alexander III, the light-cavalry unit of his choice. (The regiment was named for the Russian emperor, or czar.) After completing his required studies at the *Kriegsschule* (officer candidate school) in Berlin, he received his commission as *Leutnant* (lieutenant) in 1912. "At last I was given the epaulettes," he recalled later. "It was a glorious feeling, the finest I have ever experienced, when people called me Lieutenant." Two years later, his nation went to war.

On June 28, 1914, a fanatical Serbian nationalist assassinated Archduke Franz Ferdinand, heir to the throne of Austria-Hungary, and his wife, in the Bosnian capital of Sarajevo. The assassinations produced a chain reaction of threats and mobilizations. Old grievances and underlying animosities surfaced between the Central Powers (mainly Germany, Austria-Hungary, and Turkey) and the Triple Entente (Allied) Powers (chiefly Britain, France, and Russia— and later the United States). Barely more than a month later, in midsummer 1914, the "guns of August" announced the start of World War I.

On August 2, 1914, the day after Germany had declared war on Russia, Leutnant Manfred Baron von Richthofen led his troop of gray-clad light cavalry across the Prosna River into Russian Poland on their first combat patrol. At the outset of hostilities, the cavalry served as "the eyes of the Army." As Manfred noted later, "We young cavalry lieutenants had the most interesting task. We were to study the ground, to work towards the rear of the enemy, and to destroy important objects." Unrestrained by false modesty, the baron added, "All these tasks require real men."

The War to End All Wars

The spark that started World War I and set Europe aflame for four years in 1914 was struck in Sarajevo on the day of the St. Vitus celebration. The festivity commemorated the Battle of Kosovo (June 28, 1389) in which the Serbs suffered a humiliating defeat at the hands of their age-old enemies, the Turks. It was struck by the hand of Gavrilo Princip, a nineteen-year-old Serbian nationalist, dedicated to freeing the Balkans from the Serb-perceived yoke of Habsburg oppression. Thus, when Archduke Franz Ferdinand, heir to the Habsburg throne of Austria-Hungary, and his wife, Sophie Chotek, Duchess of Hohenburg, visited the Bosnian capital on June 28, 1914, Gavrilo Princip shot them both dead. As grim and shocking as this event was, it did not cause World War I but rather only provided an excuse for it.

Early in the 20th century, Europe was split into two armed camps—the Central Powers (chiefly Germany, Austria-Hungary, and later Turkey), and the Triple Entente (Allied) Powers (mainly France, Russia, and Great Britain—and later the United States). In this alliance-dominated hotbed of imperial, territorial, and economic rivalries, war became a virtual certainty looking for a place to happen. Austria-Hungary wanted to expand its boundaries into the Balkans. Germany sought to establish itself as the preeminent European power and to challenge Britain's claim to naval superiority.

Historically, France felt threatened by Germany, particularly since her defeat in the Franco-Prussian War (1870–71) and the resulting loss of most of the Alsace-Lorraine region. Great Britain eyed the growing naval might of Germany with alarm. And Russia, viewing itself as champion of the Slavs, hungered to expand into the Balkans and extend its borders to the sea. Nationalism lent its fierce pride to the mix of conflicting interests in both camps.

As Europe moved into the second decade of the new century, all that was needed to touch off the much written about "guns of August" was the metaphorical torch of a self-appointed executioner in Bosnia. Barely more than a month later, every major power in Europe had entered into the "war to end all wars," as the combatants and others of that generation so naively referred to it.

Manfred quartered his small troop in the little town of Kieltze (Kalisz), where he and his men spent five uneventful days. Each day, he sent a man back to regimental headquarters with a reconnaissance report. By the fifth night, his troop had winnowed down to himself and two others. After posting a sentry in the belfry of the town church, Manfred bedded down for the night, only to be awakened by his sentry's whispered voice. "The Cossacks are here," he said.

Under cover of darkness and a light, misty rain, Manfred led his two Uhlans and their horses to an open field outside town, then returned through the churchyard to the village street. It was true. About 30 Cossacks (Russian cavalrymen) were milling about noisily in the street. Manfred, recognizing that discretion is the better part of valor, slipped away with his men to a nearby wood. At daybreak, the Cossacks rode out of the village, and the three Prussians returned to their post in Ostrowo (Ostrów Wielkopolski). Manfred had learned a valuable lesson and vowed never to be caught by surprise again.

In mid-August, a call came for fast-moving cavalry to support the rapid German advance on the Western Front. Most of the heavy fighting in the east was occurring north of the First Uhlans, so Manfred's regiment soon found itself aboard a westbound train. To Manfred's dissatisfaction, his regiment was detached to an infantry unit of Crown Prince Wilhelm's German Fifth Army, near Metz, in northeastern France. Functioning as part of an infantry unit greatly reduced his chances of taking part in any classic cavalry charges.

In the meantime, Manfred's brother Lothar had entered the war as a member of the Fourth Dragoon Regiment (heavily armed cavalry) known as "Von Bredow's Own." (Adalbert von Bredow was a Prussian general who had led one of the last full-fledged cavalry actions in Europe during the Franco-Prussian War in 1870.) Unlike his older brother,

Lothar had not aspired to a military career. He had remained in the public school system in Breslau, had graduated from *Gymnasium* (high school), and was undergoing compulsory military training in Danzig (Gdansk, Poland) when the war broke out and his regiment was mobilized. When Lothar's unit was sent west to join the assault on Belgium, Manfred greatly feared that his brother would see action before him. In a letter to his mother, written in September 1914, he complained:

> I feel certain that Lothar has already been in big cavalry charges such as we will probably never ride in here. . . .
>
> I hear that a cavalry division stands on the approaches to Paris, and I nearly believe that Lothar is lucky enough to be there. But apart from that, he must certainly have seen more [action] than I have here before Verdun.
>
> The army of the Crown Prince is investing [besieging] Verdun from the north, and we must wait till the fortress surrenders.

But the fortress at Verdun did not surrender. After the First Battle of the Marne (September 5–10, 1914), the German advance ground to a halt, and World War I settled into static warfare fought in filthy trenches, dank dugouts, and water-filled shell holes. Manfred's glorious vision of war that he had spent years training for—cavalry charges at a gallop, with sabers flashing and pennants flying—had slowly faded. And when "the war of movement" ended, the need for horse cavalry ended with it.

The young nobleman was reassigned to duty as a communications officer. His duties required him to make frequent trips to the front lines through an intricate maze of trench lines under heavy fire. Although he was awarded the *Eisernes Kreuz II. Klasse* (Iron Cross, Second Class) for the risks involved, he found the task boring and yearned for a

Manfred was reassigned to duty as a communications officer—a position that brought him to the frontline of the battle, pictured here—when the need for cavalrymen faded. A subsequent string of monotonous assignments prompted him to apply for the Air Service.

chance at some real action. Manfred's subsequent assignment as *Ordonnanzoffizier* (assistant adjutant) of the Eighteenth Infantry Brigade relegated him to a desk job and continued monotony— not a choice assignment for a highly trained and increasingly restless Uhlan.

Manfred's disenchantment with his duties climaxed in May 1915 when he was reassigned again, this time as a supply officer, even farther removed from the action. He exploded. In a most unmilitary letter to the commanding general of his unit, Manfred wrote: "My Dear Excellency:

I have not gone to war in order to collect cheese and eggs, but for another purpose." He went on to officially apply for the *Fliegertruppe* (Air Service). His uncustomary application was accepted, and he received his transfer to the flying service—his passport to the clouds—at the end of May 1915.

Fate and
the Hunter

s a result of his brash request for transfer to the Air Service, Manfred was sent to *Flieger-Ersatz-Abteilung (FEA) 7*, an aviation training unit in Cologne, to assess his aptitude for becoming an air observer. He was one of thirty candidates, only the best of which would be selected for flying duty. The rest would be returned to the trenches. Manfred had seen enough of the foot soldier's war and had little desire to return to it. He soon wrote home with pride: "It is under these extremely difficult and doubtful circumstances that I, fortunately, find myself one of these selectees."

At the training facility, life returned to near normalcy for the young baron, or at least as normal as life can be for a youth in service under arms in time of war. He enjoyed dining at a regular officer's mess, wearing clean clothes every day, and sleeping between clean sheets every night. Most of all, however, he welcomed the prospect of serving once again in the kind of military unit in which he could make a more meaningful contribution to his nation's war effort. And if transferring to the Air Service improved his chances of distinguishing himself and earning more medals— as he felt sure it would—then so much the better.

Manfred's transfer to the German Air Service's training facility provided him with some of the creature comforts he missed in the trenches of the Western Front; he is seen here with his dog, Moritz. It also provided him with the opportunity he longed for—making a meaningful contribution to the German war effort.

On the eve of his first training flight, Manfred retired early, so as to ensure that he would be fresh and alert for one of the biggest events of his young life. He arose early and drove over to the flying field a little before seven o'clock. At the appointed hour of seven, he climbed "for the first time into a flying machine," a two-seater biplane trainer that would lift the future air ace into the sky for the first time. He described those first few moments in a strange new environment:

> The draught [draft] from the propeller was a beastly nuisance. I found it quite impossible to make myself understood by the pilot. Everything was carried away by the wind. If I took up a piece of paper it disappeared. My safety helmet slid off. My muffler dropped off. My jacket was not sufficiently buttoned. In short, I felt very uncomfortable. Before I knew what was happening, the pilot went ahead at full speed, and the machine started rolling. We went faster and faster. I clutched the sides of the car [fuselage]. Suddenly, the shaking was over, the machine was in the air and the earth dropped away from under me.

Manfred had been briefed on their scheduled route and was supposed to direct the pilot as a test of his observational skills. But the pilot kept zigzagging to confuse him, and he lost all sense of direction. Caught up in the thrill of his first flight, he did not mind at all. "It was a glorious feeling to be so high above the earth, to be master of the air," he wrote afterward. "I didn't care a bit where I was, and I felt extremely sorry when my pilot thought it was time to go down again." The ex-Uhlan had found a different kind of mount to ride into battle.

The importance of the airplane as a reconnaissance weapon had come into its own by 1915. Restricted by a maze of trenches that stretched from Holland to the Swiss frontier along the Western Front, the cavalry could no longer function effectively as "the eyes of the army." The advent of tethered observation balloons took up some of the void created by the cavalry's obsolescence, but their effectiveness was limited to small areas. From an airplane, however, a trained pilot and observer could see forever—or at least far enough for some military visionaries to refer to air units as "the cavalry of the clouds."

On June 10, 1915, Manfred and his fellow observer candidates reported for training to *Flieger-Ersatz-Abteilung 6* (FEA 6) at Grossenhein in the kingdom of Saxony. At FEA 6, Manfred could have applied for pilot training but opted to remain with the shorter two-week observer course to expedite his return to action. He later explained why:

> Of course I was anxious to go forward [to the front] as quickly as possible. I feared that [otherwise] I might come too late, that the world-war might be over. I should have had to spend three months to become a pilot. By the time three months had gone by, peace might have been concluded.

Eleven days later, Manfred completed his training and was "sent to the only spot where there was still a chance of a war of movement." He was sent to Russia.

On June 21, the ex-cavalryman and newly qualified air observer joined the field aviation unit *Feldflieger-Abteilungen 69*. He arrived at the front shortly after General August von Mackensen's German-Austrian Eleventh Army had smashed through the lines of the Russian Third Army at Gorlice and was attacking Rawa Ruska. During June, July, and part of August 1915, Manfred flew reconnaissance patrols for the Austro-Hungarian Sixth Army Corps nearly every morning and afternoon during the advance from Gorlice to Brest-Litovsk.

Manfred flew reconnaissance patrols over the Russian front after completing his training as an observer. General von Mackensen, pictured here, led the German-Austrian Eleventh Army to a victory at Gorlice shortly before Manfred's arrival in Russia.

Meanwhile, brother Lothar's unit had been sent back to its home base in Lüben (Lubin) to train replacements for the soldiers lost in the first eleven months of the war. By then, several of Manfred's relatives and close friends had died in the conflict. Manfred felt lucky to be in the Air Service. "I am especially happy to be right here, in the most important theatre of operations," he wrote home, "and to be able to participate in it."

The fledgling observer recognized the importance of a good pilot from the start and felt fortunate to have *Oberleutnant* (first lieutenant) Georg Zeumer as his own. Zeumer had transferred from Flanders to the Eastern Front. He had contracted tuberculosis and did not have long to live. Consequently, he had developed a devil-may-care attitude, preferring to be killed in combat than to die in bed. A French pilot would grant Zeumer his wish and shoot him down a year later. Teamed with Manfred, however, Zeumer's skill as a pilot assured his observer of a close look at many important enemy installations on the ground.

Flying low to the earth in their slow, three-bay Albatros B.II biplane entailed great risks to the airmen from enemy ground fire. But it was the best way to get the job done. And both men seemed to revel in the dangers involved. Although ideally suited to each other, their association lasted only a short while and ended with Zeumer's transfer back to Flanders. Manfred set out at once to find another pilot who could match Zeumer's skill. He found one in *Rittmeister* (cavalry captain) Erich *Graf* (count) von Holck, another former cavalry officer and a veteran pilot at age twenty-nine.

"We made many splendid reconnaissance flights—who knows how far—into Russia," Manfred recounted later. The young baron felt supremely confident flying with the older count. "When I looked into his determined face, I had even more courage than before." Notwithstanding the count's flying skills and the baron's confidence in his pilot, their last flight together almost resulted in the early end of both noblemen.

Trying to determine the strength of an enemy force, they followed in the wake of a group of retreating Russians who were torching everything in their path. As they approached the city of Wicznice, a column of black smoke rose up some 6,000 feet or more directly in front of their Albatros, which was then flying at about 4,500 feet. Manfred, in the front cockpit, motioned for Holck to fly around the towering obstacle. The count, a successful race-car driver before the war, shook him off. Manfred later recorded what ensued:

> [T]he greater the danger, the more attractive it was to him. Therefore, right into it! It was fun to be with such a plucky fellow. But our carelessness soon cost us dearly, for barely had the tail of the aircraft disappeared into the cloud [of smoke] than I noticed a swaying in the aeroplane.

The smoke stung Manfred's eyes and the surrounding air grew much warmer. Below him, he could see nothing but "an enormous sea of fire":

> Suddenly the aeroplane stalled and plunged spiralling downward. I could only grab a strut to brace myself; otherwise I would have been tossed out. The first thing I did was look [back] into Holck's face. I regained my courage, for his bearing was of iron confidence. The only thought I had was: it is so stupid to die a heroic death in such a needless way.

They did not die, of course. Their Albatros suddenly emerged from the tower of smoke and Holck regained control of it. He pulled up at about 1,600 feet and headed for the German lines, but danger still beckoned to them. Russian soldiers opened fire and hit their engine, forcing them to land in enemy territory. Fortunately for the daring pair, their own advancing troops arrived in time to rescue the downed airmen and provide horses for their safe return to base. Both men were subsequently transferred, each to a different unit.

In mid-August, Manfred was posted to the *Brieftauben-Abteilung Ostende* (the "Ostend Carrier Pigeon Unit"), a cover name for a secret unit established to pioneer long-range bombing techniques. At Ostend, a seaport in northwest Belgium, he was happily reunited with his old pilot, Zeumer. Together, they flew five to six hours every day in the twin-engine AEG G-type *Grosskampfflugzeug* (Big Combat Aircraft). They first dropped their bombs on Belgian cities and towns and on British and French airfields. Then, with Manfred armed only with a rifle in the initial phase of plane-to-plane fighting, they would seek out chance encounters with enemy aircraft.

Manfred's first taste of air combat came on September 1, 1915, when he spotted a British Farman, an awkward aircraft with the crew's nacelle (enclosure) mounted between the wings and affixed to twin booms supporting the tail elements. The Germans classified this type as a *Gitterschwanz* (lattice-tail). Zeumer headed straight for it. Never having experienced an air battle before, Manfred did not know what to expect. His heart began to pound in his ears.

"Before I knew what was happening both the Englishman and I had rushed by one another," he wrote later. "I had at most fired four shots while the Englishman was suddenly in our rear firing into our shop window [German slang for the plane's fuselage] like anything." The British observer scored several hits on the AEG. Then, for no apparent reason, the Farman abruptly broke off the engagement and turned for home. The fight ended with little damage to either combatant.

Back on the ground, Zeumer blamed Manfred's poor shooting for not hitting the British Farman. Manfred in turn laid the blame on Zeumer's inability to maneuver their aircraft into an advantageous shooting position. In the end, both men realized that they had to fight as a team and put aside their differences. But Manfred recognized from that first experience that successful air fighting required two things: good marksmanship and control of one's aircraft.

In mid-September, Manfred's unit was deployed to the German Third Army front. Zeumer began spending most of his time becoming proficient with flying the new Fokker E.III *Eindecker* (monoplane) that was racking up victories over Allied aircraft. Manfred was forced to look for another pilot and was eventually assigned to fly with Oberleutnant Paul Henning von Osterroht. An alumnus of Wahlstatt and Gross-Lichterfelde, the twenty-seven-year-old Osterroht had served not as a cavalryman but as a prewar military pilot. He vigorously exploited every chance he got to use the airplane as a weapon, a trait much to Manfred's liking.

Flying in the smaller, lighter, and more maneuverable Aviatik C.I, Manfred now manned a Parabellum 7.9-mm machine gun that he could switch between mounts on both sides of the fuselage as needed. He soon got a chance to use it.

One September day, over the front near Champagne, the new duo spotted a French Farman. Osterroht drew close to the enemy aircraft, apparently without being seen. "When I had exhausted my supply of 100 cartridges," Manfred recalled later, "I thought I could not trust my eyes when I suddenly noticed that my opponent was going down in curious spirals." The Farman crashed into a shell crater in enemy territory. Manfred's first kill went unconfirmed, and he therefore never received credit for it.

Later, regarding his unconfirmed kill, Manfred patriotically declared, "[T]he chief thing is to bring a fellow down. It does not matter at all whether one is credited with it or not." His comment seems to belie his true feelings, for he would later use every means at his disposal to gain confirmation and souvenirs of his victories—scraps of canvas, engine parts, and even machine guns off the aircraft he had downed. His many mementos turned his

A brief conversation with German flying ace Oswald Boelcke, pictured here, whet Manfred's appetite to become a fighter pilot. But his dreams of glory at the controls of a German Fokker would have to wait.

room at Schweidnitz into a virtual Richthofen museum.

On October 1, 1915, to meet changing military needs, Manfred's rapid deployment force posted him to Rethel, in northeastern France, to join another bomber unit. En route by train, he met a rising young fighter pilot, Leutnant Oswald Boelcke, who had already shot down four enemy aircraft. Along with another young pilot named Max Immelmann, Boelcke was rapidly becoming a national hero. Photographs in newspapers and periodicals had rendered his strong, rugged features readily identifiable to Germans everywhere. Manfred engaged him in conversation and asked, "Tell me how you manage to shoot them down."

Boelcke appeared amused at first. Then, realizing that his new acquaintance was serious, he replied, "Well, it's quite simple. I fly close to my man, aim well, and then, of course, he falls down." Manfred told him he tried to do likewise but his opponents did not go down when he shot at them. "You must learn to fly a Fokker yourself, then perhaps it will be better," Boelcke said. His advice made perfect sense to the young baron.

"The difference between him and me was that he flew a Fokker and I my big fighting machine [the AEG]," Manfred wrote later. He spent the rest of the long train ride to Rethel cultivating Boelcke's friendship and learning as much as he could about air fighting in a single-seat fighter plane. Manfred could not know it at that time but fate had just taken a hand in his future.

When Manfred reached his new flying field, he immediately implored his friend Zeumer to teach him to fly the Fokker Eindecker. On October 10, after twenty-five hours of instruction, he flew alone for the first time. All went well in the air, but Manfred damaged his airplane a bit with a rough landing. He kept at it, however, and his commanding officer finally agreed to send him to FEA 2 at Döberitz, near Berlin, to complete his pilot's training. Manfred qualified as a pilot on Christmas Day 1915. But his first assignment as a pilot thwarted his fondest ambition—to fly and fight alone.

After a home leave and an extended period of inclement flying weather—during which time the new pilot persuaded his brother Lothar to apply for observer training in the Fliegertruppe—Manfred returned to the front in March 1916. He reported to *Kasta 8* of *Kagohl 2* (*Kasta* is an acronym for *Kampfstaffel*, or battle squadron, which forms a part of a *Kagohl*, a *Kampfgeschwader der Obersten Heeresleitung*, or Combat Wing of the Supreme High Command. Both the squadron and the combat wing had been established during a recent organizational change in combat aviation units). Manfred, much to his displeasure, was assigned to pilot a two-seat Albatros observation plane during the great battle for Verdun in the spring of that year—dashing his dreams of flying a fast, agile fighter plane. Despite his disappointment, he made the best of his assignment: he innovated.

Manfred had learned earlier that good marksmanship and control of one's aircraft held the key to success in air fighting. He now controlled his aircraft, but his observer had the gun. The resourceful baron remedied that short-coming by ordering a second machine gun affixed to his plane's upper wing so that he could operate it from his forward cockpit and fire over his propeller. Fellow pilots joked about his makeshift gun arrangement, but Manfred had the last laugh. On April 26, 1916, he shot down his second enemy aircraft.

Patrolling over Douaumont, a fort in the Verdun sector of northeastern France, Manfred encountered a French Nieuport single-seat fighter. "I flew after him, approached him as closely as possible, and then began firing a short series of well-aimed shots with my machine-gun," he noted later. "The Nieuport reared up in the air and turned over and over." Manfred and his observer both thought that the French pilot was trying to trick them into an unadvantageous position, but the Frenchman crashed into a wood below and disappeared. A German war

Manfred qualified as a pilot on Christmas Day 1915, but his first assignment was a disappointment for him. Instead of controlling a nimble fighter like the Fokker, he piloted a two-seat Albatros observation plane.

communiqué summed up the day's action this way:

> Two hostile flying machines have been shot down in aërial fighting above Fleury, south and west of Douaumont.

Credit for one of the downed machines belonged to Manfred. Because the Nieuport had fallen behind the French lines, however, its destruction could not be confirmed. For the second time, circumstances—some might say fate—had deprived the baron of a victory. Four days later, Manfred lost a friend.

Patrolling on April 30, Manfred sighted a lone German Eindecker attacking three French twin-engine Caudron bombers some distance away over Verdun. A stiff headwind hindered Manfred's efforts to reach the scene of the action and join the battle. He could only look on helplessly as the German pilot battled valiantly. Manfred recalled the details of his countryman's courageous fight later:

> First, he shot down a Frenchman in the midst of a hostile squadron. Then he evidently had a jam in his machine-gun and wanted to return to the air above our lines. A whole swarm of Frenchmen were on him. With a bullet through his head, he fell from an altitude of 3,000 metres [9,800 feet]— a beautiful death.

An inquiring mind might wonder what motivated Manfred's curious judgment as to what constitutes "a beautiful death," particularly after he returned to base and learned that the dead pilot was his old friend from the Russian Front, Count Erich von Holck.

On June 18, the Imperial German Air Service lost another highly valued pilot. Max Immelmann, an ace with seventeen kills, shot off the propeller of his Eindecker when the interrupter gear of his machine gun malfunctioned during an air battle. Max, known as the "Eagle of Lille" (because of his continued success against the enemy in that vicinity) plunged 6,000 feet to his death. His nation and fellow pilots, especially Oswald Boelcke, mourned his passing.

To prevent any further erosion of pilot morale because of problems with the E.III monoplane, Kaiser Wilhelm II, Germany's supreme ruler, ordered Boelcke removed from flight status. Now Germany's ranking ace with nineteen victories, he was sent to the Balkans, supposedly on an inspection tour of

German and locally allied units. At the same time, Manfred's unit was transferred to the Eastern Front to help check a Russian offensive. Kasta 2 arrived in Kovel—an important rail junction in Galicia in east-central Europe (now part of Poland and Ukraine)—in early July. Manfred had yet to gain his first official victory. But the hand of fate was again about to intervene in his affairs.

"The Eagle of Lille"

Max Immelmann came to be called "The Eagle of Lille" because of his continued success over the enemy while operating in the vicinity of Douai and Lille in northern France. The son of a wealthy factory owner in Dresden, Max began his military training at the Dresden Cadet School in 1905 at the age of fifteen. After receiving his commission as a junior officer, he transferred to the reserves to study mechanical engineering at the Dresden Technical High School. When World War I broke out, Max and his brother Franz answered their nation's call for technically educated volunteers who might wish to undergo flight training.

After earning his pilot's badge and certificate, Max was posted to *Feldflieger-Abteilung 62* (Field Aviation Unit 62) at Douai in February 1915, where he began a friendly rivalry with his squadron mate Oswald Boelcke. Max began his brief—but spectacular—career flying LVG two-seaters on observation and escort patrols. In May 1915, he was moved to his squadron's single-seat fighter, the Fokker E.III *Eindecker*.

On August 1, 1915, Max notched his first victory, shooting down a British B.E.2c of the Royal Flying Corps 2 Squadron. By year's end, he had claimed six more victories. Coincidentally, Max and Boelcke both tallied their eighth victory on January 12, 1916. Soon afterward, they both received the *Orden* (or *Ordre* in French) *Pour le Mérite*—the coveted "Blue Max"—Germany's highest award for gallantry in action.

Max elevated his victory tally to 15 on May 16. His final two victories came on June 18, 1916, when he shot down two British F.E.2b pushers. During his fight with the second "Fee," the interrupter gear of his machine gun malfunctioned. Max shot off his own propeller and plummeted 6,000 feet to his death.

Max Immelmann remains famous today not so much for his many victories and innumerable awards for valor, but rather for his creation of one of aviation's most famous aerial maneuvers—the Immelmann turn—a half loop upwards followed by a roll.

In July 1916, while the war on the Western Front remained stalemated, the Air Service recalled Boelcke from his tour, promoted him to *Hauptmann* (captain), and gave him command of Jasta 2. The new fighter squadron was being formed in an attempt to regain German air dominance in the west. Boelcke was authorized to handpick his pilots. As chance would have it, Hauptmann Boelcke passed through Kovel while en route to his new command. He decided to do some recruiting there.

Boelcke remembered Manfred. On the morning of his departure, he appeared at Manfred's door wearing the *Orden Pour le Mérite* (Order for Merit)—Germany's highest award for valor—and asked him if he would like to become one of his "pupils."

"I almost hugged him when he asked me if I wanted to go with him to the Somme," Manfred wrote later. "My fondest wish was fulfilled," he continued, "and now began the most beautiful time of my life. . . . As I was about to leave, a good friend called to me: 'Don't come back without the Pour le Mérite!'" Manfred left by train for the Somme three days later.

Fate—that fickle orchestrator of human affairs—had again worked its magic. And the man born to hunt would soon set the skies ablaze in the practice of his deadly sport.

Boelcke
and Beyond

I n late August 1916, while making his way across Germany by train to his new duty station, Manfred stopped off at Schweidnitz to spend a few relaxing days with his family. While there, he went hunting with his father. Between them, they shot fifteen partridges. Within a month, Albrecht's oldest son would be stalking a far deadlier game in the skies over the Western Front. Meanwhile, significant changes were occurring in the German military structure.

On August 29, 1916, *Generalfeldmarschall* (General Field Marshal) Paul Ludwig Hans von Beneckendorff und von Hindenburg, the acclaimed overall commander of the Eastern Front, replaced *General der Infanterie* (General of Infantry) Erich von Falkenhayn as chief of the German general staff. Falkenhayn, the chief architect of the failed Verdun offensive, had allegedly requested to be relieved of command at the young age of fifty-five.

This shift of command at the top level boded well for the Air

Service, as its chief, *Feldflugchef* Hermann von der Lieth-Thomsen, was a favorite of Hindenburg's chief of staff, Erich Ludendorff. The recently promoted General der Infanterie Ludendorff had also been appointed *Generalquartiermeister* (Quartermaster General) and as such controlled the personnel and matériel allocated to the Air Service. Oswald Boelcke, in turn, was a favorite of Lieth-Thomsen.

In addition to being an outstanding fighter pilot, Boelcke was a pioneer of combat aviation tactics—the skillful maneuvering of aircraft in battle—an advocate of formation flying, and, in the opinion of many, the father of the German Air Service. His advanced theories would now command the attention they deserved. The free-ranging but tactically ineffective fighter units operating at the time in the west

Wilhelm II is seen here marching with Generals Hindenburg and Ledendorff. When he was promoted to Generalquartiermeister, Ludendorff favored the Air Service's chief, Lieth-Thomsen, with personnel and matériel.

needed reorganizing if they were to regain dominance over the rapidly increasing and improving Allied air forces.

After Max Immelmann's death, Boelcke had written a paper entitled "Air Fighting Tactics" that he forwarded to the German High Command, and which later became the "bible" of German fighter pilots. The paper caught the eye of Kaiser Wilhelm II, who liked what he saw. He authorized Boelcke to reorganize the German fighter forces and do whatever was necessary to fix the existing shortcomings of the German fighter command.

Boelcke set to work at once with his usual dedication. As Lieth-Thomsen noted, "[T]he reports on tactical, technical and organization questions . . . which Boelcke continually gave me, formed a unique and valuable basis for the official battle orders drawn up by my staff." Boelcke quickly organized Jagdstaffeln, each composed of six fighter planes (increasing to twenty-one later in the war). The mission of the Jastas was to escort and defend the slower observation and bomber aircraft, and to search out, engage, and destroy enemy aircraft. Boelcke took command of Jasta 2—which had been officially founded on August 10, 1916—and his handpicked pilots. Twenty-four more Jastas would be formed by the end of the year.

On September 1, 1916, Manfred Baron von Richthofen arrived at Bertincourt, on the Somme Front. Over the next several weeks, other pilots straggled in to the home of Boelcke's new Jasta to fill out its roster. They included *Leutnant der Reserve* (Reserve Lieutenant) Erwin Böhme, the oldest member of the group at age thirty-seven; Leutnant Max Ritter von Müller, a veteran reconnaissance pilot who, like Manfred, sought more action as a fighter pilot; and Leutnant der Reserve Hans Reimann, a friend of Manfred's from Kasta 8.

While waiting for new and improved aircraft to arrive, Boelcke established a daily routine that enabled him to perform the dual task of continuing his combat flying without interruption and of training his pilots in air fighting techniques that he had learned over the Western Front. Every morning at dawn he flew a solitary combat patrol. When he returned, he would join his fledgling fighter pilots over breakfast and hold a class in fighter tactics. Each afternoon, he would lead his pilots into the friendly skies over

 ## Boelcke's Dicta

In the summer of 1916, at the request of German Air Service chief Hermann von der Lieth-Thomsen, Oswald Boelcke summarized the principles that should govern every air fight. His brief dicta, expressed in simple terms, remained in effect for the remainder of the war. They were:

- Try to secure advantages before attacking. If possible, keep the sun behind you.
- Always carry through an attack when you have started it.
- Fire only at close range and only when your opponent is properly within your sights.
- Always keep your eye on your opponent, and never let yourself be deceived by ruses.
- In any form of attack it is essential to assail your opponent from behind.
- If your opponent dives on you, do not try to evade his onslaught, but fly to meet it.
- When over the enemy's lines never forget your own line of retreat.
- Attack on principle in groups of four or six. When the fight breaks up into a series of single combats, take care that several do not go for one opponent.

[Boelcke's dicta have been widely published. For verification purposes, see Johannes Werner, *Knight of Germany: Oswald Boelcke German Ace*. Trans. Claud W. Sykes. Novato, CA: Presidio Press, 1985, pp. 183–184.]

Bertincourt to apply lessons learned in the morning. As his novices elevated their fighter skills, Boelcke began bringing them along on his "hunting flights"—the ultimate test of their ability.

Manfred's turn came on September 17, 1916. By then, Boelcke had increased his victory tally to twenty-six. He selected Manfred and four others to accompany him. Jasta 2 took to the air as a complete unit for the first time in six newly arrived Albatros D.II fighter planes. The single-seat biplane was armed with twin, fixed Spandau LMG 08/15 machine guns. Because of the aircraft's rounded propeller spinner and overall sleek lines from nose to tail, pilots soon nicknamed the Albatros D-types "*Haifisch*" (shark).

"We were all beginners, [and] none of us had until now been credited with a success," Manfred wrote later. "Whatever Boelcke told us was taken as gospel. . . ." All of the pilots struggled to stay close behind their trusted mentor. "It was clear to all of us that we had to pass our first test under the eyes of our revered leader," the baron added.

Only minutes into their flight, Boelcke and his fledgling pilots arrived over the front and sighted an enemy formation of eight B.E.2c biplanes of 12 Squadron, RFC, and six F.E.2b pushers of 11 Squadron heading toward Cambrai. The sharp-eyed Boelcke spotted them first and led his squadron mates into battle. But since his main purpose that day was to watch his pilots in action, he held his fire at first and maintained a position from which he could protect one of his novices who might forget in the heat of the fray to look behind him for an enemy on his tail. Manfred and the others picked a target and attacked.

Manfred chose an F.E.2 piloted by Second Lieutenant Lionel B. F. Morris of 11 Squadron. He opened fire on the Englishman and missed, then banked sharply to avoid return fire from Morris's observer, Lieutenant Tom Rees. Manfred maneuvered behind and below the enemy aircraft unseen.

"I was animated by a single thought: 'The man in front of me must come down. . . .'" he wrote later. He fired a lethal burst at the Fee's engine at point-blank range. Continuing, he recounted the results of his marksmanship:

> I was so close to him that I was afraid I would ram into him. Then, suddenly, the opponent's propeller turned no more. Hit! The engine was shot up and the enemy had to land on our side, as it was out of the question for him to reach his own lines.

Manfred had shattered the Fee's engine and wounded both Morris and Rees, but Rees managed to land his aircraft intact near Villers Plouich. The elated baron followed his victim down to confirm his kill, bumped to a rocky landing, and arrived at the downed aircraft just in time to watch the removal of its dead observer and dying pilot. Manfred then flew back to Bertincourt, about six miles away, and joined his Jasta mates for a late breakfast. When asked what had taken him so long, he replied proudly, "One Englishman shot down!" Manfred Baron von Richthofen had scored his first official victory.

On his Jasta's first day out as a group, Hauptmann Boelcke found ample cause to rejoice. Besides Manfred's victory, Leutnant Erwin Böhme had notched his first victory, a Sopwith two-seater, and Leutnant Hans Reimann had knocked down his second, an F.E.2b. Once Boelcke felt confident that his pilots had positioned themselves well, he had found the time and opportunity to shoot down an F.E.2b himself, his twenty-seventh kill. All in all, Jasta 2 had gotten off to a pretty fast start.

That night, Manfred wrote to a jeweler in Berlin and ordered a small silver cup about two inches high and an inch across, inscribed "1. Vickers 2. 17.9.16," which connoted his first victory, scored over a "Vickers-type" two-seater, on

Manfred's first victory was on September 17, 1916 in a dogfight with the British. He shot down a "Vickers-type" two-seater—it would be the first of many confirmed victories.

September 17, 1916. He sent it home, because a hunter must show off his trophies. For Manfred—hunter extraordinaire— there would be many cups to follow.

On September 23, Boelcke again led five comrades on a hunting patrol over the road between Bapaume and Cambrai.

Near Bapaume, they encountered a flight of six British Martinsyde G.100 "Elephant" single-seaters from 27 Squadron, RFC. Manfred singled out one of them and claimed his second victim. His combat report that day read: "Adversary dashed, after 300 shots, mortally wounded, near Beugny (Street Bapaume-Cambrai) to the ground."

Manfred's friend Hans Reimann also bagged an "Elephant" for his fourth victory, then went after another flown by Lieutenant (later Air Marshal) Leslie F. Forbes. Out of ammunition, Forbes deliberately rammed Reimann's Albatros. Reimann crashed to his death just north of Beugny. Forbes limped home to fight again.

That night, Manfred ordered another silver cup from his jeweler in Berlin, a ritual that continued until a silver shortage in Germany ended the practice with Manfred's sixtieth kill in September 1917.

On September 24, a dense morning haze dampened prospects for combat flying. Jasta 2 used the down time to start relocating to a new field in Lagnicourt, some nine kilometers (5.6 miles) north of Bertincourt. The move was intended to spread German airfields more evenly throughout the Somme sector. Manfred now began knocking down enemies at a rate of about one a week—an F.E.2b on September 30, a new British single-seat B.E.12 biplane on October 7, another on October 16, and still another on October 25.

Meanwhile, a general reorganization of the entire German Air Service occurred on October 8. The *Fliegertruppe* (Air Service) yielded to the *Luftstreitkräfte* (Air Force) to consolidate all aviation-related units, and to concentrate on developing tactics and strategies (plans for an entire operation or campaign) for massed air strength. *Generalleutnant* (Lieutenant General) Ernst von Hoeppner was appointed *Kommandierende General der Luftstreitkräfte* (Commanding General of the Air Force). Eighteen days later, on October 26, Boelcke upped his victory total to forty. Then tragedy struck the squadron.

On October 28, 1916, after a day's respite from the fighting because of inclement flying weather, Boelcke and his eagles answered a late-afternoon call for help from the German lines during a British infantry attack near Flers. Boelcke, as usual, led Jasta 2 to the front. "We always had a wonderful feeling of security when he was with us," Manfred wrote afterward. "After all, he was the one and only."

Over Flers, the Jasta met two B.E.2d two-seaters from 5 Squadron, RFC. Boelcke attacked one. Manfred maneuvered above the tail of the other and commenced firing. But he was forced to pull off when one of his mates flew between him and the "impertinent" Englishman. Manfred then watched from a distance of about 200 yards as his leader and his opponent circled each other to gain the advantage. Then, suddenly, the unthinkable happened. Later, in a letter home, Boelcke's good friend Erwin Böhme recounted his part in the tragic event:

> Boelcke and I had just got one Englishman between us when another opponent, chased by friend Richthofen, cut across us. Quick as lightning, Boelcke and I both dodged him, but for a moment our wings prevented us from seeing anything of one another—and that was the cause of it.
>
> How am I to describe my sensations from the moment when Boelcke suddenly loomed up a few metres away on my right! He put his machine down and I pulled mine up, but we touched as we passed, and we both fell earthwards. It was only just the faintest touch, but the terrific speed at which we were going made it into a violent impact.

Böhme's machine incurred only light damage to its landing gear, but his friend's aircraft lost the extreme tip of its left wing.

Manfred described the tragedy's conclusion in a letter to his mother on November 3:

> At first, Boelcke went down normally. I followed him immediately. Later one of the wings broke away and he went rushing down. His skull was crushed on impact; therefore he died instantly. It affected us all very deeply— as if a favourite brother had been taken from us.

Thus died the great Boelcke. He was given a funeral fit for a reigning prince, as indeed was his due. Oberleutnant Stefan Kirmaier, the squadron's senior officer and an ace with six victories, succeeded Boelcke as commander of Jasta 2. After six weeks of air fighting, Jasta 2 casualties numbered six dead and one wounded. Two men had suffered nervous break- downs. But the war went on. Manfred had shot down his seventh foe—an F.E.2b—on that very day. He ended his letter stating, "My nerves have not yet suffered as a result of the others' bad luck."

The blond, steely, blue-eyed killing machine continued to add silver cups to his collection at a steady pace, scoring four more victories in November and another four in December. After his eighth victory on November 9, over a B.E.2c, His Royal Highness Duke (Carl Eduard) of Saxe-Coburg-Gotha awarded him the *Ovale Silberne Herzog Carl Eduard-Medaille* (Oval Silver Duke Carl Eduard Bravery Medal). And two days later, the army announced that he had been awarded the Knight's Cross of the Royal Order of the House of Hohenzollern with Swords. The medal was generally considered to be a prerequisite toward receiving the highest honor of all, the Pour le Mérite. Manfred's fame was spreading.

The epic Battle of the Somme ended in miserable weather on November 18, 1916, but Jasta 2 kept fighting. Leutnant der Reserve Werner Voss, another former cavalryman, joined the squadron on November 21, a day before *Staffelführer* (squadron

These French Flyers are celebrating the downing of enemy aircraft during the Battle of the Somme. This battle was costly for the British, who lost some 60,000 soldiers in a single day of the offensive.

leader) Stefan Kirmaier was shot down while seeking his 12th victory. (A succession of squadron leaders followed Kirmaier as head of Jasta 2, which would be renamed Jasta Boelcke in December.) Voss, a worthy addition to the Jasta, would soon rival Manfred as a national figure and a consummate air fighter. Two days later, Manfred set an example for Voss.

One of the Manfred's most famous aerial duels occurred south of Bapaume on November 23, 1916. His name was just beginning to resonate in the airy arena above the trenches when the gods of war matched him against one of Britain's best—Major Lanoe George Hawker of 24 Squadron, RFC.

Hawker, an experienced pilot, had learned to fly before the war. His name became a household word in Britain when he bombed the German Zeppelin (dirigible) sheds at Cologne from the dangerously low height of 200 feet. Britain awarded him the Distinguished Service Order (DSO) for "conspicuous gallantry" for his action. He later became the first British pilot to shoot down three enemy planes in one day, a deed for which he won the Victoria Cross (VC), Britain's highest award, for his "most conspicuous bravery and very great ability."

His running battle with Manfred began when he broke off from a flight of three D.H.2 single-seat pusher-type fighters. "The Englishman tried to catch me up in the rear while I tried to get behind him," Manfred wrote in his diary later. "So we circled round and round like madmen after one another at an altitude of about 10,000 feet. First we circled twenty times to the left, and then thirty times to the right." Each man maneuvered to gain the upper hand, struggling to command a position above and behind the other.

Hawker labored to overcome two distinct disadvantages: a west wind that blew him steadily eastward as the battle went on, and an aircraft that was technically inferior to his opponent's aircraft. In the hands of a less skillful pilot, Hawker's D.H.2 would have provided no match for the baron's new Albatros D.II., which was perhaps the best fighter flying at the time. So the contest between two masters of their art continued, all the while moving farther eastward and dropping lower and lower in altitude.

"When we had got down to about 6000 feet without having achieved anything particular," Manfred went on, "my opponent ought to have discovered that it was time for him to take his leave." But he did not. The battle by then had drifted eastward as far as Bapaume, about a half-mile behind the German lines. "The gallant fellow was full of pluck," noted Manfred, "and when we had got down to about 3000 feet he merrily waved to me as if to say, Well, how do you do?"

Their circles narrowed to no more than 250 to 300 feet across. Manfred recalled looking down into Hawker's nacelle and observing every movement of his head. Only his helmet prevented the baron from seeing his facial expressions. "My Englishman was a good sportsman, but by and by the thing became too hot for him," Manfred declared. "He had to decide whether he would land on German ground or whether he would fly back to the English lines."

Hawker's two companions had already left for home. One had been damaged in a fight with another German; the other had lost sight of him. Not wanting to remain over enemy ground alone, Hawker elected to make a dash for it before he ran too low on fuel. Manfred had waited patiently for this "most favorable moment." His diary recorded the end of his classic encounter with Hawker this way:

> I followed him at an altitude of from 250 feet to 150 feet, firing all the time. The Englishman could not help falling. But the jamming of my gun almost robbed me of success.
>
> My opponent fell shot through the head 150 feet behind our lines. His machine-gun was dug out of the ground and it ornaments the entrance of my dwelling.

Manfred claimed his 13th and 14th victories—a D.H.2 and an F.E.2d respectively—on December 20. Then, through luck and manipulation, he arranged to spend Christmas with his father and brother Lothar at Jasta Boelcke's new airfield at Pronville, five kilometers (3.1 miles) from Lagnicourt. Lothar, like Manfred, had soon tired of flying as an observer and had transferred from Kasta 23 into pilot training school the previous summer. The retired fifty-seven-year-old Albrecht, who had volunteered to return to active duty as a major, joined his sons from a small garrison that he commanded near Lille. The Richthofen warriors shared a joyful reunion.

The next two days provided the Richthofens with additional cause for celebration: Lothar soloed for the first time on the 26th; and Manfred shot down his 15th foe—an F.E.2b—on the 27th. In a letter to his mother, Manfred stressed Lothar's achievement and declared, "Now the next big event will be [his] first aerial victory." That event would not take long in coming.

Manfred closed out 1916—and the two months beyond the death of his revered mentor Oswald Boelcke—with 15 kills, maintaining his stunning average of a victory every week. And the young nobleman from Silesia was just getting started.

"Bloody April"

F our days into the new year of 1917, Manfred scored his 16th victory. It came over a Sopwith "Pup" of 8 Squadron, Royal Navy Air Service (RNAS). The Pup, a forerunner of the famous Sopwith "Camel"—made even more famous in recent years by Snoopy in Charles Schulz's beloved comic strip *Peanuts©*—was a new British contestant in the aerial arena. "I managed to get behind him and shot him down," Manfred logged in his combat report for January 4. "The plane broke apart whilst falling." The new British machine was to be his last victory as a member of Jasta Boelcke.

On January 14, 1917, in recognition of his leadership and achievements, Manfred was appointed commanding officer (CO) of Jagdstaffel 11. His new squadron was quartered on the German Sixth Army Front at an airfield just outside Douai and northeast of Arras. Manfred felt less than delighted over his appointment. "I must say I was annoyed," he admitted later. "I had learnt to work so well with my comrades of Boelcke's squadron, and now I had to begin all over again working hand in hand with different people. It was a beastly nuisance." At the same time, he understood the importance of the appointment to his career.

Manfred was awarded the *Orden Pour le Mérite* after shooting down his sixteenth enemy aircraft. He joined the ranks of flying aces Oswald Boelcke and Max Immelmann, who received the award one year earlier.

Two days later, a telegram arrived from German Head-quarters that helped to relieve any misgivings that he may have felt over leaving Jasta Boelcke. Simply stated, it read: "His Majesty, the *Kaiser*, has awarded the *Orden Pour le Mérite* to *Leutnant* von Richthofen." The award bore the date of January 12, 1917, precisely one year after the same honor had been authorized for Oswald Boelcke and Max Immelmann.

A notice distributed to Sixth Army air units declared that Manfred's award was for "the successful confirmed downing of 16 enemy aeroplanes." Earlier, the award of the Pour le Mérite had required only eight confirmed kills, but as the war progressed and the scores of German pilots increased, so too did the number of kills needed for the award.

Before leaving Jasta Boelcke, Manfred had been one of the first pilots to receive one of the new Albatros D.IIIs. He took it with him to his new airfield at La Brayelle, just northwest of Douai. Shortly after taking command of Jasta 11, Manfred hit upon the idea of painting his aircraft all red, ostensibly as a taunt to his enemies. "The result was that everyone got to know my red bird," he noted later, adding, "My opponents also seemed to have heard of the colour transformation."

Actually, Manfred had experimented with various camouflage color schemes and found them to be ineffective: from below, an aircraft's distinct silhouette still stood out sharply against the sky; and from above, earth-colored camouflage became useless above the clouds where most air battles were fought. Manfred's all-red machine gave rise to his colorful sobriquet "the Red Baron" and might even have worked to his advantage, serving as a warning to his enemies and an inspiration to his friends.

Nonetheless, his squadron mates became concerned for his safety when news reached them that the British had put a price on their leader's head. Brother Lothar (who would join Jasta 11 in March) explained later how Manfred's pilots reacted to the British bounty:

> Every flyer on the other side knew him, for at the time he alone flew a red-painted aeroplane. For that reason it had long been our wish to have all aeroplanes of our *Staffel* painted red and we implored my brother to allow it so he would not be so especially conspicuous.

Manfred granted their request, but insisted that all other planes in the squadron must have some additional marking in another color. He reserved the sole right to an all-red aircraft. Since the pilots could not see one another's faces, they used the added color as identifiers. Continuing, Lothar wrote:

> [Leutnant Karl Emil] Schäfer, for example, had his elevator, rudder and most of the back part of the fuselage [painted] black; [Leutnant Karl] Allmenröder used white [on the nose and spinner], [Oberleutnant der Reserve Kurt] Wolff used green and I had yellow. Each one of us was different.

Other Jastas soon followed the lead of Jasta 11. Because of their splash of gaudy colors, and because of their tendency to move often from airfield to airfield, British pilots dubbed the German squadrons "flying circuses"—and another legend was born.

As soon as he arrived at La Brayelle, Manfred began molding himself and his new command in the image of Erwin Boelcke, emulating the professional demeanor of his departed mentor, and teaching, employing, and refining his tactics. On January 23, he led six of his pilots to a hunting sector over the trenches near Lens to introduce them to his brand of air fighting. Just prior to their arrival at Lens, Second Lieutenant John Hay of 40 Squadron, RFC, had shot down two Albatros two-seaters. Manfred took him on and made short work of the Englishman and his F.E.8 pusher aircraft. The baron's combat report for the day read in part:

> The plane I had singled out [Hay's] caught fire after 150 shots, fired from a distance of 50 metres [55 yards]. The plane fell, burning. Occupant fell out of plane at 500 metres [1,640 feet] height.

Manfred's conquest of Hay marked his 17th victory and Jasta 11's first. Both numbers were about to increase dramatically. Manfred claimed another Englishman the next day—an F.E.2b west of Vimy—to end January with 18 kills. The victory also came close to ending the baron's string of victories when a cracked lower wing forced him into an impromptu landing. Manfred was not injured, but because of a structural defect in the new D.IIIs, they were grounded until modifications corrected the flaw. In the interim, he had to fly a single-seat Halberstadt D.II—an early successor to the Eindecker—while adding a dozen subsequent victories to his string.

Poor flying weather and the administrative duties of command slowed him down in February, limiting his victories to three B.E.2d two-seat biplanes. As the weather improved, however, so also did Manfred's toll of victims. Ten more enemies fell to his guns in March: seven two-seaters—a Sopwith 1 1/2 "Strutter," five B.E.2s, and an F.E.2b pusher; and three one-seaters—a D.H.2 pusher, a SPAD SVII, and a Nieuport 17. The SPAD and Nieuport fighters reflected the growing improvement in Allied aircraft quality.

On March 9, as if to remind the seemingly invincible baron of his mortality, his borrowed Albatros D.III (factory-fresh after undergoing structural modifications) took a hit in its fuel tank during an engagement with an F.E.8 of 40 Squadron, RFC. His engine quit and the Albatros headed straight down. Describing his descent later, Manfred wrote, "I am leaving behind me a trail of white mist. I know it very well [from having seen it in] opponents. It happens just before an explosion." The D.III did not explode. Manfred landed it safely in a meadow where a comrade picked him up. The baron returned to the air within the hour to claim his 25th victim, a badly outclassed D.H.2.

On March 22, Manfred received word that he had been "promoted by order of the *Kabinett* [Royal Cabinet of Ministers] to Oberleutnant." Barely more than two weeks later, he received word of his promotion to *Rittmeister* (cavalry captain) on April 7. His captaincy came through the cavalry in keeping with army tradition. As the commander of Jasta 11, Manfred could dictate his own flight schedule, and he flew as often as possible. But the demands of leadership, such as the staffing and training of his squadron, occupied a lot of his time during February and March.

In World War I, Germany experienced a chronic shortage of qualified young men for the air service. But Manfred, as one of Germany's *gross Kanonen* (great flying aces), could request the services of promising airmen who caught his attention and the Air Force would honor his request. In this way, he staffed Jasta 11 with such quality pilots as Leutnant Karl Allmenröder, Oberleutnant der Reserve Kurt Wolff, and Leutnant Karl Emil Schäfer, all future aces, recipients of the Pour le Mérite, and Staffel leaders. Perhaps the pilot whom Manfred wanted the most—and got—was Leutnant Lothar Freiherr von Richthofen.

Lothar arrived at La Brayelle on March 10, a blustery Saturday unfit for flying. Manfred introduced him around the squadron just as he would any other new arrival. The younger Richthofen received no favors or special treatment from his brother, except, perhaps, when Manfred assigned him to one of his old machines—a Halberstadt D.II—in which he had scored ten victories. On March 28, flying his brother's old "crate," Lothar shot down his first enemy aircraft, an F.E.2b from 25 Squadron, RFC. Lothar went on to knock down nine more enemies in the Halberstadt to equal his "big" brother's feat. And he did it in just 12 days during the month that aviation history records as "Bloody April."

Beginning in January 1917, French General Robert Georges Nivelle, the supreme commander of the Allied forces, had started planning for a great spring offensive in the Champagne sector. At about the same time, the Germans had unknowingly foiled his plans by withdrawing their forces in the Champagne area to stronger defensive positions along the Siegfried (or Hindenburg) Line. The line ran from Arras in the north to just east of Soissons in the south. Nivelle's impending offensive caused a stir of air activities in the vicinity of Arras as Allied planes flew continual patrols over the German lines to observe enemy movements. German Jastas were intent on denying their observations.

The ground battle for Arras, the prelude to Nivelle's offensive, began on April 9, 1917; the air battle over Arras started five days earlier. On April 4, the British had some 25 RFC squadrons, supported by RNAS fighter units, concentrated near Arras. This positioned them directly opposite Jasta 11, at Douai. By April, the Germans had assembled 37 Jastas that they could bring to bear against the Allies. But these figures are deceptive. In actual aircraft numbers, some 754 British planes, including 385 single-seat fighters, faced 264 German aircraft, of which 114 were single-seat fighters.

During the five days before the start of the Second Battle of Arras (April 9-15, 1917), the Germans shot down 75 British airplanes. Over the course of 27 days in April—the worst of 52 months of war for British pilots—the British lost 151 aircraft and 316 airmen killed in action. German losses totaled 70 aircraft.

Two factors weighed heavily in tipping the balance of victories and losses so drastically in favor of the Germans in April 1917: first, the British practice of spreading their more experienced pilots evenly—but thinly—across their frontline squadrons, as contrasted with the German preference for concentrating their best pilots in elite units such as Jastas 2

General Robert Georges Nivelle, supreme commander of the Allied forces, planned an offensive in the Champagne sector for the spring of 1917. The offensive was to be preceded by a ground battle for the Arras and a flurry of air battles dominated by the Germans.

and 11; second, the superiority of German aircraft in performance and firepower.

With regard to pilot dispersion, elite German squadrons

overwhelmed their less-experienced adversaries, while unseasoned German units held their own against British squadrons with few veteran air fighters. In the second instance, although the British introduced new aircraft designs in April, they came too late and too few in number to make a difference. (Two quality aircraft that made their debuts in April were the Sopwith Triplane, the first Allied fighter to mount two synchronized machine guns, and the S.E.5, which rivaled the Sopwith Camel as the most successful British single-seat fighter of the war.) The Germans, with the Richthofen brothers in the forefront, ruled the skies in April 1917—the month that the United States entered the war.

On April 11, Manfred shot down a B.E.2c of 13 Squadron, RFC, to chalk up his 40th victory, equaling the mark of his

 ## Sopwith Camel

The Sopwith Camel, probably the most famous fighter plane used during the First World War, was designed around a twin, forward-firing installation of Vickers machine guns. Mounted on top of the otherwise smooth engine cowling, the noses of the twin gun barrels barely cleared the propeller blades. A humped fairing covering the twin gun butts in front of the pilot gave rise to the unofficial and unflattering name of "Camel."

For the most part, the Camel's performance ranked less than spectacular. But its lightning-like response in the hands of a skillful pilot set it apart from its peer aircraft and earned the Camel an enduring place in aviation annals. Nothing could stay with a Camel in a tight, left-hand turn. Because of the over-balancing effect of its rotating engine, however, the Camel often slid into a flat spin during a tight turn. More than a few Camels crashed to earth in this manner.

Hated by pilots unschooled in her whims, yet loved by pilots who mastered her tricky ways, the Sopwith Camel rightfully ranked as the first choice of fighting machines among the best Allied fighter pilots.

SPAN: 28 feet. LENGTH: 18 feet, 9 inches. ENGINE: 130 hp Clerget. ARMAMENT: two Vickers machine guns. MAXIMUM SPEED: 115 mph at 6,500 feet. SERVICE CEILING: 19,000 feet.

mentor Boelcke and earning him the distinction of Germany's greatest living fighter pilot. That same day, Lothar bagged two enemies.

Six days earlier, the British had initiated night bombing raids on Jasta 11's field at La Brayelle. High-level German commanders recognized the danger to their prized air fighters—and to the Richthofen brothers, in particular. So, in mid-April, once again in gray, drizzly weather, they moved the squadron to an airfield at the town of Roucourt, 6 kilometers (3.7 miles) southeast of Douai. A little farther from the front, the new Teutonic Knights of the Air would be less likely to die ignoble deaths on the ground, and the commanders could rest more easily. But there was no rest for the pilots of Jasta 11.

Manfred shot down his 44th aircraft on June 14—a Nieuport 17 single-seater—to become the ranking Ace of Aces among all the warring forces. Four times during that bloody month, Lothar shot down two British planes in one day. He scored one of his double victories on April 29, a day on which the senior Richthofen was visiting Roucourt from his garrison in nearby Lille. Albrecht arrived at the airfield just as his sons were returning from an early morning patrol. Lothar jumped out of his aircraft and greeted his father proudly. "Hello, Papa," he said. "I have just shot down an Englishman."

Manfred joined them. "We had breakfast with [father] and then flew again," he said. He might have added, *and again, and again, and again.*

At the end of the day, Manfred, with four victories, had upped his score to 52–21 in April alone. Lothar shot down a second British plane, his 14th in April, to bring the combined Richthofen score on the 29th to six. Manfred did not fly again in April, but Lothar claimed one more enemy victim on the 30th. Of the 151 British aircraft losses that month, the Richthofens together accounted for 36 of them. And so ended "Bloody April."

Shattered Myth

A t nine o'clock in the evening on the last day of April 1917, Manfred received an important telephone call from the German High Command. "They gave me over the wire the cheerful news that His Majesty [Kaiser Wilhelm II] had expressed the wish to make my personal acquaintance," Manfred recalled later, "and had fixed the date for me." He had been ordered to take a leave after surpassing Boelcke's record of 40 with his 41st victory on April 13, but he had not wanted to miss any of the action over Arras. Now seemed like as good a time as any to take leave from the front.

Manfred's audience with the Kaiser had been set for May 2. It was impossible for him to reach German Army headquarters at the Rhineland hot springs and resort city of Bad Kreuznach in time by train. The *Kurhaus* (German for "cure house"), an elegant spa and casino complex, had become the imperial residence. By chance,

Leutnant der Reserve Konstantin Krefft, his unit's technical officer, happened to be flying home on a convalescent leave in a two-seater on May 1. Manfred arranged to fill the second seat of the "big, fat two-seater" with Krefft serving as his pilot-chauffeur.

Neither the end of April nor Manfred's absence would cause hostilities to cease, of course, so Staffelführer von Richthofen left another Richthofen in charge of Jasta 11, his brother. Although Kurt Wolff, a high-scoring ace with 26

Kaiser Wilhelm II, seen here at German General Headquarters with Hindenberg and Ludendorff, arranged to meet Manfred in person in May 1917. Their meeting would include a lunch, at which Wilhelm gave Manfred a birthday present and offered him praise for his victories.

victories, appeared to be the logical choice to fill in for Manfred temporarily, Manfred recognized the public relations — some say propaganda—value of keeping a Richthofen in charge of his "flying circus." Moreover, Manfred wanted to see how Lothar would act on his own—outside the long shadow cast by Germany's leading air fighter. Manfred transferred the leadership of Jasta 11 to Lothar with a simple handshake on May 1 and left on leave.

Even as he traveled to a hero's welcome at the Kurhaus, Lothar was leading a combined flight of aircraft from Jastas 3, 4, 11, and 33. The massed fighter formation represented a change of German air fighting tactics authorized by Air Force commander Generalleutnant Ernst von Hoeppner. Lothar bagged an F.E.2b, his 17th victory, on May 1. Over the next 13 days, he would shoot down seven more foes to bring his total to 24.

Meanwhile, at Bad Kreuznach, Manfred met first with Generalleutnant Ernst von Hoeppner, then with Generalfeldmarschall Paul von Hindenburg and a host of dignitaries, and finally with General der Infanterie Erich von Ludendorff, mostly to discuss the military situation. At noon on May 2, he lunched with Wilhelm II. "It was my birthday and someone must have divulged that to His Majesty and so he congratulated me," Manfred recalled afterward. "First on my success, then on my twenty-fifth year of life. He also surprised me with a small birthday present."

The emperor's rather immodest gift was a bronze and marble bust of himself in military attire that took two stout servants to carry into the dining room. Manfred had it shipped home to Schweidnitz where it took its place among the growing accumulation of honors conferred upon him by his grateful nation. Despite the self-glorifying aspect of giving a bust of himself, the Kaiser's gift—a lasting symbol of the German state—seems ironically fitting to the occasion: It was the last birthday of Germany's greatest hero.

Manfred left Bad Kreuznach on May 4—the same day that Kurt Wolff became the 18th fighter pilot to receive the Pour le Mérite—to spend several days hunting at the state game preserve at Freiburg in the Black Forest. From Freiburg, he wrote to his mother on May 9, informing her of his itinerary:

I am shooting pheasants here and expect to remain here until the fourteenth. The sport is wonderful.

After that, I have to go to Berlin to look over the new planes. That will take me about three days, and then for Schweidnitz.

Manfred's plans further called for him to tour the other fronts toward the end of the month, to help boost the morale of Central Powers airmen fighting on the Eastern Front and in the Balkans. Four days later, a curt telegram from the front interrupted his sporting pleasures. "Lothar is wounded, but not mortally," it said, nothing more. Lothar and Karl Allmenröder had attacked and downed two enemy two-seaters within British territory earlier that day—Lothar's 24th victory and Allmenröder's 12th. But Lothar, flying low to the ground, had been struck in the right hip by ground fire on his long return flight to Roucourt.

Manfred followed up on his brother's situation and received two more telegrams the next day. One said: "Your brother is in satisfactory condition at the hospital in Douai, according to a telephone inquiry made today by your Staffel." The second one declared: "Today your brother has been awarded the *Orden Pour le Mérite* by His Majesty." Now satisfied that Lothar was not in mortal danger, Manfred remained on leave, content in the belief that German air mastery at the front would continue unabated. He was wrong.

New British pilots and aircraft were starting to arrive at the front in droves. The new British machines included the

S.E.5 single-seat fighter, the Bristol F.2A two-seat fighter, and the D.H.4 two-seat fighter-bomber. All of these new models soon showed themselves a match for German Albatroses and Halberstadts. Furthermore, rumors of thousands of Americans undergoing accelerated air-training courses for both the British and French air services were running rampant among frontline Germans. As the summer of 1917 drew near, the Allies were gradually regaining control of the air over the front.

The Nivelle Offensive petered out in mid-May, but British Field Marshal Douglas Haig was already planning a new offensive in Flanders, in northwest Belgium. He was determined to break through the German lines between the North Sea and the Lys River. Haig selected the Ypres salient—a protrusion in the German lines—as his point of attack. Success of his offensive hinged upon first driving the Germans off the dominating high ground at Messines Ridge. Preparatory to the Battle of Messines (June 7, 1917), British artillery pounded the ridge for 17 days, and the Royal Flying Corps seized control of the air.

On June 5, Leutnant Karl Emil Schäfer—now the commander of Jasta 28—and others of his squadron attacked an F.E.2d of 20 Squadron, RFC, over Zandvoorde. Schäfer, who had earned the Pour le Mérite and other honors in April, had just scored his 30th victory the day before. The twenty-six-year-old ace would not claim another. He went down under the guns of the two-seater's veteran crew. His comrades sent his body to his home in the town of Krefeld in Westfalia. Manfred interrupted his leave again to attend Schäfer's funeral. He then went on to Berlin to prod his contacts in the Directorate of Military Aviation into producing a successor for the outmoded Albatros fighters.

The Albatros line—even the new Albatros D.V series—continued to experience structural problems and were already inferior to the latest Allied models. And, so far, the new German massed-fighter formations had proved ineffective. In the

These German soldiers await orders to join the front in Flanders. Manfred cut his leave short and rejoined his squadron when the British started attacking in Flanders in June 1917, and trained his pilots in the new Albatros D.Vs.

eyes of Manfred's superiors, the deteriorating situation over the trenches required his return to the front. On June 10, with the British attacking in Flanders, they recalled Manfred from leave.

Manfred returned to his squadron a few days later. During his absence, Jasta 11 had moved from Roucourt to Harlebeke, in northwest Belgium near Courtrai, to draw closer to the new battle lines. Leutnant Karl Allmenröder, while filling in for Manfred as acting Staffel leader, had become the squadron's fourth recipient of the Pour le Mérite. Manfred's job now became one of elevating other Staffel members to Allmenröder's level of proficiency. Their new location was far enough removed from the battlefront to enable Manfred and his pilots to spend hours over Harlebeke familiarizing themselves with their new, recently delivered Albatros D.Vs without fear of hostile intrusions.

On June 18, Manfred, confident that his airmen were ready for battle, led them on morning and afternoon patrols. During the afternoon patrol, Manfred attacked an R.E.8 of 9 Squadron, RFC, north of Ypres. From up close, he fired 200 shots into the body of the two-seater. "Without falling immediately, the plane went down in uncontrolled curves to the ground," he reported later. "Driven by the wind, it fell into Struywes's farm, where it began to burn." The master had not lost his touch.

That night, Manfred wrote to "*Liebe* [Dear] Mamma" to tell her of his fifty-third victory. He also conveyed some sadder news. "Yesterday, Zeumer was killed in air combat," he penned. "It was perhaps the best that could have happened to him. He knew he had not much longer to live." It was for that reason that Manfred had denied Zeumer's request to join Jasta 11. He had, however, recommended him for a transfer to Jasta Boelcke, where Zeumer died fighting. "As it is," Manfred concluded, "he died a heroic death before the enemy." The baron's words suggest in this letter and in other writings the kind of end that he might choose for himself.

Manfred, as if he had never taken time out to go on leave, followed with three more victories in June—a Spad VII single-seat fighter on the 23rd, a D.H.4 two-seater on the 24th, and an R.E.8 two-seater on the 25th. His combat report for the 25th reads:

> I was flying together with Leutnant Allmenröder. We spotted an enemy artillery flyer whose wings broke off in my machine gun fire. The body crashed burning to the ground between the trenches.

Two days later, Leutnant Karl Allmenröder, whom Manfred had designated to succeed him as Staffelführer of Jasta 11, answered the ultimate call himself. On June 27, Allmenröder, holder of the Pour le Mérite and victor in the air over 29 opponents, fell to earth and crashed after his aircraft was struck by antiaircraft fire over Zillebeke. He was twenty-one years old. In a letter to Karl Allmenröder's father, Manfred wrote: "I myself cannot wish for a more beautiful death than to fall in aerial combat; it is a consolation to know that at his end Karl felt nothing."

 ## Special Ammunition

With rare exceptions, airmen of both the Allied and Central Powers during World War I used regular ammunition in their operations until the middle of 1916. It then became clear to both sides that regular ammunition was not effective in destroying lighter-than-air craft. An incendiary alternative was needed that would ignite gas-filled kite-balloons that were used for artillery spotting and observation. This need led to the introduction of special ammunition in the summer of 1916.

"Special" ammunition consisted of three basic types of bullets: incendiary, explosive, and expanding.

The incendiary bullet was derived from the already existing tracer bullet, a bullet containing a phosphorus charge that enabled the shooter to "trace" the bullet's path to its target. Far more dangerous than the tracer, the soft-nosed incendiary bullet contained an incendiary charge at its base. It would flatten out and ignite upon striking an object.

The explosive bullet, as its name implies, exploded on contact, thereby inflicting far more damage than regular bullets on both airman and aircraft.

The expanding bullet, or dumdum, with either a split or hollow-point nose, broke apart and flattened out upon impact. An antipersonnel munition by design, its severe maiming effects on humans caused both sides to back off from its use.

Both incendiary and explosive bullets saw increasing use over the last two years of the war. Although used primarily against observation balloons, they were also used to a lesser extent against aircraft. The number of aircraft going down in flames increased steadily and significantly during 1917 and 1918. It seems fair to say that the use of special ammunition might have had something to do with the increase of flamed aircraft.

On July 2, not long after the formation of Jagdgeschwader 1 (JG 1) on June 24, the new air wing concentrated its four squadrons in new quarters at Markebeke. As *Geschwader-Kommandeur* (Wing Commander) of JG 1, Manfred guided the fortunes of the unit that many aviation historians feel was the first true—if not the original—flying circus. He claimed his 57th victory that same day—an R.E.8 of 53 Squadron, RFC.

"The RE reared up [after his first shots] and I fired on the rearing aircraft from a distance of 50 metres [55 yards] with a few more shots until flames shot out of the machine and the opponent crashed burning," he reported. It was a proper example for his subordinates in a command that had recently quadrupled in size.

According to Air Force commander von Hoeppner, the massive flying unit owed its existence to the buildup of RFC units in increasingly greater strength:

> The ever-increasing number of aircraft which the opposition deployed to reach a target made it seem desirable for us to combine several *Jagdstaffeln* [fighter squadrons] into a *Jagdgeschwader* [fighter wing]. . . . In the personage of *Rittmeister* von Richthofen . . . the *Geschwader* received a *Kommandeur* whose steel-hard will in relentlessly pursuing the enemy was infused in every member of the *Geschwader*. His refined lack of pretension, his open, gallant manner [and] his military skill secured for him amongst the Army an unshakeable trust that, despite his young age, was matched with great respect.

Small wonder that the baron's pilots, without exception, would have followed him anywhere. On the bright, clear morning of July 6, 1917, two of them did.

While leading a scouting patrol of his "gentlemen" from Jasta 11 (now headed by Leutnant Kurt Wolff), Manfred met a flight of six F.E.2d pusher biplanes of 20 Squadron, RFC,

When a British fighter opened fire on Manfred's plane at an impossible 300 yards, he thought he had nothing to fear—until he was hit in the head by a stray bullet, blinded, and sent hurtling towards the earth. Manfred miraculously survived, and is seen here recovering by his father's side.

midway between St.-Omer and Bailleul. The lead British aircraft was crewed by flight leader Captain Donald Charles Cunnell and observer Second Lieutenant Albert Edward Woodbridge. Manfred singled out their two-seater and flew straight at it, head-on. Woodbridge opened fire on him from a distance of 300 yards. Manfred felt no concern. At so great a distance, he thought, "the best marksmanship is helpless." But, as he found out abruptly, there is no accounting for random hits. In the baron's words:

> Suddenly, something strikes me in the head. For a moment, my whole body is paralyzed. My arms hang down limply beside me; my legs flop loosely beyond my control. The worst was that a nerve leading to my eyes had been paralyzed and I was completely blind.

It does not take a pilot to understand the gravity of being alone and blind in an airplane high in the air. And the baron's predicament grew steadily worse. His machine tumbled out of control. He waited anxiously, expecting his wings to break off. "This is how it feels when one is shot down to his death," he thought.

He soon regained power over his arms and legs, and he could grip the wheel. He never lost consciousness, and his presence of mind told him to cut his engine. But his blindness persisted. He forced his eyes open but still could not see, not even the sun. And down he fell. To the sightless airman, "seconds seemed like eternities. . . . One can't fly without sight." He must regain his sight—or die.

Then, as if he had willed it so, his sight began to return, dimly at first, as though he were "looking through thick black goggles." He looked first at his altimeter and managed to right his powerless Albatros before he ran out of height. As his vision cleared, a shell-scarred and wooded landscape appeared below him. He recognized that he was within his own lines and attempted a landing amid the shell craters. "I landed my machine without any particular difficulties," he wrote later, although he "tore down a few telephone wires, which, of course, I didn't mind at the moment."

Manfred tumbled out of his machine but found himself too weak to rise again. Nearing unconsciousness, he looked up to discover that two of his comrades—Leutnants der Reserve Otto

Brauneck and Alfred Niederhoff—had followed him down to cover his landing. Fortunately, he had landed beside a road near Wervicq, Belgium. A motor ambulance soon arrived and rushed him off to St. Nicholas's Hospital in nearby Courtrai, where doctors treated a head wound that would keep him out of action for some time.

"I had quite a respectable hole in my head," Manfred wrote later, "a wound about ten centimetres across which could be drawn together later; but in one place clear white bone as big as a *Taler* [large-size coin] remained exposed. My thick Richthofen head had once again proved itself." His most urgent concern lay in his quick return to the front. "I am curious as to who can climb into the crate first," he wrote, "my brother or I."

Both Richthofen brothers would return to the bloody skies over Western Europe to claim many more victories. But on a bright, clear morning in July, the myth of the Red Baron's invincibility had been shattered forever.

Becoming
Immortal

Oberleutnant Kurt von Döring, leader of Jasta 4, filled in for Manfred as acting Geschwader-Kommandeur, while the baron spent the next three weeks recuperating physically from his head wound and psychologically from his narrow escape from death.

Later in the day on July 6, Oberleutnant Karl Bodenschatz, Manfred's adjutant (administrative officer), and three of his Jasta leaders visited him in the hospital at Courtrai. They wanted first-hand information about his condition. Although they found their leader pale and drawn, Manfred managed a few encouraging words. "I am very sorry to be away right in the middle of things," he said, "but I will be back again, very soon." Starting early the next morning, Oberleutnant von Döring led the pilots of JG 1 on a day of vengeance patrols, in which they shot down nine enemy aircraft without a loss.

Four days later, the Geschwader suffered another significant loss. Leutnant Kurt Wolff, leader of Jasta 11, was wounded in the left shoulder and hand during a fight with twelve Sopwith Triplanes over Ypres. Wolff managed to land his Albatros intact but his wounds would keep him out of action for more than a month while he convalesced in the same hospital with Manfred. Oberleutnant Wilhelm Reinhard took charge of Jasta 11.

Manfred rejoined JG 1 on July 25. Still not fully recovered, he would not regain sufficient strength to fly again until mid-August. Three weeks in the hospital had perhaps allowed him more time than he might have wanted to reflect on the war and on his role in it. The deep crease in his skull left an even deeper gash in his psyche, which, arguably, he never

The Sopwith Triplane fighter was designed to give British pilots the widest field of vision and increased maneuverability. Leutnant Kurt Wolff, leader of Jasta 11, would learn the effectiveness of this design when he was wounded in a battle with 12 Sopwith Triplanes.

completely overcame. The British bullet had changed him, perhaps reawakening in him a sense of his own mortality.

Manfred's mother recognized the change in her son. In a later conversation with Floyd Gibbons, the baron's first biographer of note, she told him:

> Manfred was changed after he received his wounds. I noticed numerous differences in him. His fears for Lothar's safety increased, and he was no longer certain that victory would come to our side. He said that people in Germany did not realize the power of the Allies as well as did the men who had to face their forces at the front.

Manfred had always dreaded growing old. In his adult life, he lived perpetually in the near-presence of death and seemed to nurture a sense that he would die young. Not wishing to leave a widow behind, he refused to marry, even though strong evidence exists that he loved a young maiden in Berlin. His actions and demeanor almost suggest a man in a rush to pierce the veil of mystery that separates the living from whatever lies beyond. Did he suffer depression? Probably. Did he overcome it? Absolutely.

The war was not going well for Germany. No one knew that better than Manfred. Driven by a fierce patriotism and an iron will, he returned to the aerial arena long before the restorative power of time could heal him completely in body or in spirit. He was not finished yet. Manfred had made one inexcusable error by flying straight at his enemy and allowing him a clear shot. He would make one more mistake—a mistake that would cost him his life. But in his few remaining months, Germany's Red Baron would work hard at becoming immortal.

Upon his return to Marckebeke, Manfred brought good news to his subordinates: Jagdgeschwader 1 was to be reequipped with the new Fokker triplane. Noted designer Anthony Fokker had designed the contentious little airplane as a pure fighting machine, capable of outshooting and out-flying any of the opposition aircraft. Manfred described it as "manoevrable as the devil," which would enable his pilots to "climb like monkeys." It was needed, as British opposition from Sopwith Camels, S.E.5s, and Bristol fighters kept growing heavier and fiercer with each passing day.

On July 30, Leutnant Werner Voss joined JG 1 as a replacement for Jasta 10 leader Oberleutnant Ernst Freiherr

Fokker Dr.I Triplane

In the summer of 1917, while recuperating from a head wound, Manfred von Richthofen wrote to a friend serving on the staff of Ernst von Hoeppner, commanding general of the German Air Force. Richthofen complained that the quality of Allied fighter aircraft had eclipsed that of German fighters. "English single-seaters climb better and are faster than us," he wrote, "and the English even have already [the Bristol fighter], a two-seater, that can overhaul an Albatros, easily overpowering us in turns, against which one is virtually powerless." With German losses rising and German pilot morale declining, Richthofen demanded a new aircraft that could regain control of the air over the Western Front. The German high command called upon the noted Dutch aircraft designer Anthony Fokker to create such an airplane, and the Fokker Dr.I triplane roared off his drawing board.

Fokker based his "new" design on the Sopwith Triplane, thus the concept was not actually new. But it was a fast way of producing a small, highly maneuverable machine that was nimble enough to twist and turn and quickly gain the advantage in a dogfight at lower altitudes. Although slower than either the Sopwith Camel or the S.E.5, it was light on the controls, and only a fearless foe would attempt to outmaneuver it. Rather than mix it up with a Dr.I, British pilots generally chose to attack it by diving and quickly zooming out of harm's way.

Despite early structural problems with the Dr.I that caused the deaths of several pilots, Richthofen grew to love the little plane and scored his last seventeen victories in it.

SPAN: 23 feet, 7 inches. LENGTH: 19 feet. ENGINE: 110 hp Oberusel. ARMAMENT: two Spandau machine guns. MAXIMUM SPEED: 115 mph ground level. SERVICE CEILING: 19,600 feet.

von Althaus, who was gradually growing blind. Voss, now a Pour le Mérite recipient and Manfred's closest rival for scoring honors with 34 victories, constituted a welcome addition to the new air wing. Earlier that month, he had been recalled to Berlin from the front to test-fly the Fokker V4 prototype triplane, a testimonial to his brilliant flying skills. Voss arrived just in time. The following day, Anglo-French forces attacked along the Flanders Front, announcing the start of the Third Battle of Ypres (or Passchendaele), a battle that would carry into November and cost both sides huge losses—nearly 309,000 Anglo-French and some 260,000 German casualties.

Leutnant Kurt Wolff returned to Marckebeke on August 7, but he was unable to resume even nominal command of Jasta 11. Like Manfred, Wolff required more time to recuperate before he could fly again. Oberleutnant Wilhelm Reinhard remained in charge of Wolff's old squadron.

Manfred finally returned to the air on August 16. Though still weak and not entirely well, he engaged a new Nieuport 28 single-seat fighter from 29 Squadron, RFC, over Ypres. "I shot up his engine and fuel tank," he reported later. "The aeroplane went into a tail spin." He followed it down and watched his 58th victim augur into the ground. Ten days later, he bagged a SPAD VII from 19 Squadron, RFC, near Ypres.

The first two triplanes—designated F.I—arrived at Marckebeke on August 28. Flying a triplane for the first time four days later on September 1, he targeted an R.E.8 artillery-reconnaissance aircraft over Flanders. "I approached and fired twenty shots from a distance of 50 metres [55 yards], whereupon the adversary fell out of control and crashed this side [of the lines], near Zonnebeke," he logged in his combat report. "Apparently the opponent had taken me for an English Triplane, because the observer in the machine stood upright without making a move for his machine gun." The Red Baron had reached the 60 mark. He ordered his 60th—and last—silver cup from Berlin.

On September 3, 1917, Manfred led five members of Jasta 11 on patrol. South of Bousbecque, on the German side of the lines, he engaged a Sopwith Pup single-seater in his Fokker triplane. After a long dogfight, he forced it to land. "I was absolutely convinced I had a very skilful pilot in front of me," he reported later, "who even at an altitude of 50 metres [164 feet] did not give up, but fired again, and opened fire on a column of troops while flattening out, then deliberately ran his machine into a tree." He came away from his 63rd kill also convinced that his Fokker F.I was "undoubtedly better and more reliable than the English machine."

Although Manfred had added four more victories to his total after his release from the hospital, it became clear to his superiors that he was not yet fit for combat duty. They ordered him to take a convalescent leave. On September 6, he left for a hunting sabbatical in the Saxon Duchy of Thuringia, as the guest of Carl Eduard, the Duke of Saxe-Coburg-Gotha —the young nobleman who had first awarded him a high honor. On that same day, Leutnant Werner Voss claimed his 42nd victory. The opportunity to catch up with Manfred's record now presented itself to Voss.

Leutnant Kurt Wolff resumed command of Jasta 11 on September 11. The next day, he received a telegram informing him that Kaiser Wilhelm II had promoted him to Oberleutnant in recognition of his notable achievements as a fighter pilot. On September 15, Wolff congratulated Leutnant Georg von der Osten on attaining his third kill. Then, flying Manfred's triplane, Wolff led his pilots into a skirmish with Sopwith Camels near Nachtigal. Osten witnessed the end of his Staffelführer. Wolff, victor over 27 foes, went down for the last time at the age of twenty-two.

During Manfred's absence in September, Leutnant Werner Voss upped his total to 48 victories, but on September 23 his luck ran out. In a classic clash with a flight of Sopwith Camels containing no less than seven British aces, the hopelessly

Leutnant Werner Voss was tallying victories and coming close to Manfred's record before being shot down and killed by a British ace. His death was difficult for his fellow pilots.

outnumbered Voss finally fell victim to the marksmanship of Second Lieutenant Arthur P. F. Rhys-Davids. Of Voss, British ace Major James B. McCudden later said, "His flying was wonderful, his courage magnificent and in my opinion he is the bravest German airman whom it has been my privilege to see fight." Voss was twenty years old.

Voss's death devastated his fellow pilots, but the return of Lothar von Richthofen to the Geschwader two days later helped to lift their spirits. Manfred, in a hurried note to his mother on September 30, wrote, "I am immensely pleased about Lothar's sudden recovery. After my leave, together we can again make it hot for the Englishmen, [as] I am in the same *Staffel* with Lothar."

Manfred, tired of the leisure and celebrity of enforced leave, returned to the front where he belonged on October 23. At Marckebeke, to his delight, he found that a new Fokker Dr.I triplane (the production model of the little machine) was being readied for his use. Manfred's elation turned to concern when a series of bizarre incidents started to cast doubt upon the highly touted aircraft.

First, mistaking a Dr.I being flown by *Vizefeldwebel* (Sergeant Major) Josef Lautenschlager of Jasta 11 for a Sopwith Triplane, an unidentified German pilot shot down and killed Lautenschlager on October 29.

Then, the next day, Manfred and Lothar flew together for the first time in more than five months, both in their new triplanes. Heavy clouds and mist restricted visibility, but Manfred observed Lothar's triplane start to behave erratically, as if trying to break apart, then start to glide downward. The baron followed his brother down. Lothar found a clear, flat spot near Zilverberg, in Flanders, and executed a perfect landing. But when Manfred tried to land, he fell victim to "some kind of damned treachery" and crashed. He emerged unscathed, but his Fokker was totally destroyed in a seemingly minor accident.

Finally, a day later, Leutnant der Reserve Günther Pastor was flying a Dr.I north of Moorsele, Belgium, when its top wing structure collapsed. The little plane plunged to earth, and Pastor died instantly on impact. On November 2, the Dr.I was grounded until an investigation by a special commission could determine the cause of the little triplane's structural problems. Meanwhile, JG 1 pilots flew either Albatroses or the new Pfalz D.III biplanes, until structural modifications on the Dr.I enabled its reinstatement at the end of the month.

On November 20, the British launched a tank offensive for the first time ever to open the Battle of Cambrai (November 20–December 6, 1917). At battle's end, some 45,000 troops on both sides had fallen. In midbattle, Manfred received the sad news of the death of Leutnant der Reserve Erwin Böhme of Jasta Boelcke. Böhme, survivor of a collision with Oswald Boelcke and by then an ace with 23 victories, was shot down by an AFWK.8 of 10 Squadron, RFC, over Zonnebeke.

Manfred and Lothar tallied two more victories each in November. The Richthofen brothers finished the year with 63 and 26 victories, respectively. Between them, they would shoot down 31 more enemy aircraft in 1918.

In January 1918, Manfred paid a final visit to his home in Schweidnitz. By then, he had become far more than a German idol and had achieved a cult status that reached far beyond the simple hero worship once accorded to Boelcke and Immelmann. At home, Manfred's mother saw the price that he had paid for his fame. She saw how dreadfully the war had transformed him.

No longer could she see in him the gay, carefree, frolicsome qualities that had lent him his boyish charm. "He was taciturn, distant, almost unapproachable," she recalled. She saw only hardness and pain in his eyes. When reminded of a dental appointment, she heard him say, "Really, there's no point." Soon afterward, Manfred returned to the front.

During the winter of 1917–1918, Generalfeldmarschall Paul von Hindenburg and General der Infanterie Erich von Ludendorff agreed that Germany needed to launch an all-out offensive on the Western Front in 1918. They intended to wrest victory from the Allies before the power of the United States could be brought to bear, in which case they felt that a German defeat would become inevitable. The question of a German offensive became not one of if but one of when. At 0440 on March 21, 1918, the booming of German guns along the Somme River in France provided the answer.

Manfred and the men of Jagdgeschwader 1, now quartered in an airfield at Cappy on the Somme, awoke to the thunder of those guns. Over the past eight days, Manfred had added three more kills to his total to bring it to 66. Brother Lothar had also added three kills to his score, upping it to 29. Then, for the second time, Lothar fell to an enemy's guns on March 13. His resultant injuries were slight but sufficient to keep him out of action until July.

During the last eight days of March, Manfred scored eight more victories to finish the month with 74. Few students of martial affairs would deny that the Red Air Fighter had already staked a claim to immortality—but he was still not done.

The Two Deaths
of the Red Baron

During the first three months of 1918, Manfred's demeanor changed perceptibly. Always a loner by nature—a characteristic that belied his superlative grasp of teamwork in air fighting—he began to absent himself more often from group gatherings, preferring to spend more and more time alone in his room. Manfred never displayed any outward signs of fear. Only conjecture can speak to what anguished thoughts that might have tormented him in the solitude of his room, or to what horrific nightmares that might have deprived him of sleep's temporary asylum from the clamor and hurt of war.

Manfred's performance as a master air fighter and leader remained exemplary. He continued to pile up victories while teaching his subordinates how he did it. Like his mentor Boelcke, Manfred developed his own set of rules for air fighting. "Never shoot holes in a machine," he told his pilots. "Aim for the man and don't miss him. If you are fighting a two-seater, get the observer first; until you have silenced the gun don't

During his final days, Manfred became withdrawn, alienated from his colleagues, and obsessed with his enemies' fiery deaths. However, he remained an exemplary fighter pilot and continued to add victories to his record.

bother about the pilot." The bullet-ridden bodies of most of his conquests attested to the ruthless effectiveness of his simple rules.

Notwithstanding his continued success, Manfred had changed. His comrades and subordinates began noticing his frequent comments on the number of adversaries he had shot down in flames. And they witnessed his growing obsession with the notion of death by fire. Was this the kind of death that he envisioned for himself? they wondered. No one will ever know. But ample evidence supports his obsession with fire.

On April 2, 1918, he shot down his 75th enemy aircraft, an R.E.8 of 52 Squadron, RAF. (A day earlier, the British Parliament had merged the Royal Flying Corps and the Royal Navy Air Service to form the Royal Air Force, or RAF.) Manfred's combat report noted:

> From ten metres [11 yards] range I shot him until he began to burn.
>
> When the flames shot out, I was only five metres [5.5 yards] away from him. I could see how the observer and pilot were leaning out of their plane to escape the fire. The machine did not explode in the air but gradually burnt down. It fell uncontrolled to the ground where it exploded and burnt to ashes.

Ludendorff's Somme Offensive lost momentum and ground to a halt on April 5, but Manfred's string of victories and obsession with fire continued. The next day, he shot down a Sopwith Camel of 46 Squadron, RAF. "The English plane which I attacked started to burn after only a few shots from my guns," he logged in his report. "Then it crashed burning near the little wood north-east of Villers-Bretonneux, where it continued burning on the ground."

Credit him with victory number 76—and another victim consumed by fire.

On April 7, Manfred shot two more Sopwith Camels out of the air for his 77th and 78th victories. One Camel disintegrated in midair, the other British plane smashed to pieces when it hit the ground. Neither aircraft burned. Two days later, Ludendorff began his second great offensive of the spring—the Lys Offensive (April 9–17, 1918). But Manfred did not mark another score until April 20 when he shot down two more Sopwith Camels of 3 Squadron, RAF.

"I put myself behind the adversary and brought him down, burning, with only a few shots," he wrote of his 79th victim. "The enemy plane crashed down near the forest of Hamel where it burned further on the ground." Three minutes after his first kill, he attacked the second Camel. "I approached him as near as possible when fighting and fired 50 bullets until the machine began to burn," he reported. "The body of the machine was burned in the air, the remnants dashed to the ground, north-east of Villers-Bretonneux." The baron had tallied his 80th victory. He would not score another.

On April 21, morning came to Cappy airfield shrouded in a dense fog. The watery blanket perhaps came as a blessing, as the pilots of JG 1 had celebrated Manfred's 80th victory far into the previous night. Manfred himself had probably celebrated in moderation in his usual fashion. Rumors had begun to circulate about his possible retirement now that he had reached a nice even number of victories. But Manfred quite likely had already targeted the loftier and more desirable even number of 100. In any case, the mists began to clear in midmorning, and Manfred and the pilots of Richthofen's Flying Circus started preparing for flight.

At about 1030, a telephone call alerted Jadgeschwader 1

that the British were over the front. Minutes later, Manfred's all-red Fokker Dr.I and five other brightly colored triplanes rose out of Cappy airfield and headed toward the valley of the Somme.

Over the front, the circus master and his followers soon sighted the enemy below them—a section of R.E.8s of 3 Squadron, AFC (Australian Flying Corps). Cruising at about 7,000 feet, the Australian aircraft were beginning a routine reconnaissance mission. Four triplanes plummeted to the attack, but the R.E.8s rushed into a protective cloud bank. When the Fokkers regrouped, they found themselves over the British lines and taking fire from below.

Earlier, the same fog that had settled in at Cappy had also blanketed the airfield of the RAF's 209 Squadron at Bertangles, delaying the start of its high offensive patrol over the Somme. Flying at 12,000 feet, eight Sopwith Camels—led by Canadian Captain Arthur Royal "Roy" Brown—approached the scene at about the same time that aircraft from Jasta 5 joined Manfred's formation. Brown's flight flew to meet the Germans. Manfred's group turned to greet the British. Moments later, the crowded sky erupted in a blaze of color, as the pilots and planes of both sides engaged again in the practice of their deadly art. They painted the sky blood red.

Canadian Lieutenant Wilfred R. May, one of the Camel pilots, was experiencing his first combat flight. Flight commander Brown had instructed him not to mix it up in a general dogfight. Rather, he was to hang around on the fringe of any action and wait for a target of opportunity to present itself. May obeyed his leader. When a Fokker broke away from the melee, May attacked it. But in his excitement, he fingered the triggers of his guns too long and they jammed. The neophyte pilot, again obeying Brown's instructions, broke off the fight and raced for home.

May did not become aware of Manfred's presence on his tail until he heard the rattle of the baron's machine guns. Twisting in his seat for a rearward look, May saw the dreaded, all-red triplane and the black-helmeted head of its occupant. May instinctively kicked hard on his rudder and jammed the control stick over. The Camel skidded across the sky in a steep turn, but the red triplane stuck fast to its tail. May tried everything he knew to shake off his pursuer, but nothing worked. Manfred pursued the elusive May for several minutes just above the Somme.

Down to a height of 200 feet, Manfred fired short bursts at the Camel, ripping holes in its wings and sending water geysers up from the river. May was about to become "cold meat," and he thought about plunging his Camel into the Somme. But he survived the chase to later say:

> Just near Corbie von Richthofen beat me to it and came over the hill. At that point I was a sitting duck; I was too low down between the banks to make a turn away from him. I felt that he had me cold, and I was in such a state of mind at this time that I had to restrain myself from pushing the stick forward and diving into the river, as I knew that I had had it.

But he had not. Fate, in the person of Captain Roy Brown, intervened.

Brown had witnessed the predicament of his fledgling combat pilot from high above. Diving to his rescue, Brown arrived just in time. With Manfred's triplane squarely in his sights, he fired a stream of bullets that stitched a trail along the red plane's fuselage. Manfred snapped his head rearward, and Brown caught a quick glimpse of the baron's expression beneath his goggles. It appeared to be one of startled horror. An instant later,

Germany's greatest ace slumped sideways in the cockpit.

At about the same time, May looked around to see the red triplane do a "spin and a half and hit the ground." The little red plane bounced and skidded to an upright halt, as if at the hand of its pilot, in an area held by Australian troops two miles behind the lines. Several Australian infantrymen rushed to the crash site and found a dead German pilot frozen to the plane's controls. Blood trickled from the baron's mouth and oozed from an exit wound in his chest. A single bullet had done its deadly work.

Manfred had made his second—and last—mistake. He had violated one of his own general principles: "One should never obstinately stay with an opponent who, through bad shooting or skilful turning, one has been unable to shoot down, when the battle lasts until it is far on the other side and one is alone and faced by a greater number of opponents." The violation cost him his life.

Initially, Captain Roy Brown received credit for shooting down World War I's leading ace in an air fight. Later, however, investigators discovered that Manfred might have fallen victim to a less noble death from ground fire.

Two Australians—Sergeant C. B. Popkin and Gunner R. F. Weston—of the Twenty-fourth Machine-Gun Company, had fired off a long burst at Manfred's triplane as it flew low over the trenches in pursuit of May. Moreover, a few seconds later, Gunners W. J. Evans and R. Buie, of the Fifty-third Battery, Fourteenth Australian Field Artillery Brigade, also fired on the triplane with their Lewis antiaircraft guns. Eventually, all these men claimed credit for downing Manfred.

Today, interested parties continue to debate the two possible versions of his death. After long years of study and conjecture, strong evidence suggests that Sergeant Cedric Bassett Popkin deserves the honor, if such recognition can be so called. But at this late date, history will probably

Manfred was shot down and killed on the Somme battlefield in 1918, and remained buried there until 1925 when he was brought back to his fatherland and laid to rest at the Invaliden Cemetery in Berlin.

The Four Burials of Manfred von Richthofen

On April 22, 1918, the day after Manfred's death, members of 3 Squadron, Australian Flying Corps, buried him with full military honors in a small cemetery in Bertangles, France. A cross fabricated from a four-bladed R.E.8 propeller marked his grave site.

Manfred rested at Bertangles until 1925 when his remains were disinterred and moved to the German military cemetery at Fricourt, France, the final resting place of some 18,000 German soldiers killed in World War I.

At the request of the Richthofen family in mid-1925, Manfred's body was again exhumed and returned to Germany on a special train for a formal state funeral in Berlin. Manfred's mother wanted to rebury him in the Schweidnitz cemetery, beside the graves of his father, who died in 1920, and his brother Lothar, who died in an airplane crash in 1922. But she recognized the right of Manfred's grateful nation to honor him properly in its own way. On November 20, 1925, following an elaborate state funeral presided over by Reich President Paul von Hindenburg, Manfred's remains were interred among numerous other German military heroes and commanders in Berlin's Invaliden Cemetery.

In 1976, at the Richthofen family's request, Manfred's coffin was removed again, this time to western Germany for a fourth—and final—burial in a family plot in Mainz. His remains now rest near those of his mother, who died in 1962; his sister Ilse, who died in 1963; and his brother Bolko, who died in 1971.

never surrender irrefutable proof of who killed Germany's Red Baron.

REQUIEM

On the morning following Manfred's death, a lone British airplane soared low over the baron's airfield at Cappy. The pilot dropped a receptacle containing a photograph of a British funeral party firing a farewell salute over a solitary grave in the cemetery at Bertangles, France. A note accompanied the photograph. It read:

> TO THE GERMAN FLYING CORPS:
>
> Rittmeister Baron Manfred von Richthofen was killed in aerial combat on April 21, 1918. He was buried with full military honours.
>
> From the BRITISH ROYAL AIR FORCE

On July 9, 1918, Oberleutnant Hermann Göring assumed command of Jadgeschwader 1 and remained at its head for the rest of the war.

Oberleutnant Lothar Freiherr von Richthofen survived the war with a final total of 40 victories. He continued flying after the war and was killed in a flying accident on July 4, 1922.

1741

November 6   King Friedrich II of Prussia (Frederick the Great) elevates the Richthofen family to the baronial ranks.

1892

May 2   Manfred von Richthofen born in Breslau, in Silesia region of Germany.

1894

September 27   Lothar von Richthofen (Manfred's brother) born in Breslau.

1903   Manfred enrolls as a cadet in military school at Wahlstatt (Legnickie Pole).

1911   Manfred graduates from the prestigious Royal Prussian Military Academy at Gross-Lichterfelde, near Potsdam.

1912   Manfred commissioned as a *leutnant* (lieutenant) of cavalry.

1914

June 28   Archduke Franz Ferdinand, heir to throne of Austria-Hungary, and wife are assassinated in Bosnian capital of Sarajevo.

August 1   Germany declares war on Russia; Europe enters World War I.

August 2   Manfred leads light cavalry troop into Russian Poland on their first combat patrol.

September 5–10   First Battle of the Marne; the "war of movement" ends.

1915

May   Manfred transfers into the German Air Service.

June 10   Manfred reports for training at *Flieger-Ersatz-Abteilung 6* at Grossenhein in kingdom of Saxony.

June 21   Manfred joins field aviation unit *Feldflieger-Abteilungen 69* as an observer.

August 15   Manfred is posted to the *Brieftauben-Abteilung Ostende* (the "Ostend Carrier Pigeon Unit") at Ostend, Belgium.

September 1	Manfred experiences first taste of air combat but fails to shoot down his opponent.
October 1	Manfred is posted to Rethel, in northeastern France, and meets rising young Oswald Boelcke en route.
October 10	Taught to fly by a friend, Manfred solos for first time.
December 25	Manfred qualifies as a pilot.

1916

June 18	Max Immelmann is killed in airplane crash.
September 1	Manfred joins *Jasta* (fighter squadron) *2* on the Somme Front.
September 17	Manfred scores first confirmed victory.
October 8	The *Fliegertruppe* (Air Service) is merged into the *Luftstreitkräfte* (Air Force) to consolidate all aviation-related units.
October 28	Oswald Boelcke is killed in midair collision with Erwin Böhme.
November 9	His Royal Highness, Duke (Carl Eduard) of Saxe-Coburg-Gotha, awards Manfred the *Ovale Silberne Herzog Carl Eduard-Medaille* (Oval Silver Duke Carl Eduard Bravery Medal); two days later, Manfred receives the Knight's Cross of the Royal Order of the House of Hohenzollern with Swords.
November 23	Manfred shoots down British ace Lanoe George Hawker.
December 26	Lothar von Richthofen solos for the first time.
December 27	Manfred shoots down an F.E.2b to end the year with 15 victories.

1917

| January 14 | Manfred is appointed commanding officer of Jasta 11. |
| January 16 | Manfred is awarded the *Orden Pour le Mérite*—the "Blue Max"—Germany's highest award for valor in combat. |

March 10	Lothar joins Jasta 11.
April	"Bloody April"; Richthofen brothers together shoot down 36 enemy aircraft.
April 13	Manfred scores 41st victory to surpass Boelcke's record of 40.
April 9–15	Second Battle of Arras.
May 2	Manfred visits Kaiser Wilhelm II.
May 13	Lothar is shot down and wounded.
June 18	Manfred shoots down his 53rd enemy aircraft.
June 24	*Jadgeschwader* (fighter wing) *1* formed, known to many as Richthofen's Flying Circus.
July 2	Manfred claims 57th victim.
July 6	Manfred is shot down and wounded over Comines-Warneton and is hospitalized for three weeks.
July 25	Manfred rejoins JG 1.
September 3	Manfred bags 63rd kill.
November	Manfred and Lothar tally two more victories each to finish year with 63 and 26 victories, respectively.

1918

March 13	Lothar is again shot down.
March 21–April 5	German Somme Offensive.
March 23	Manfred promoted to *Oberleutnant* (first lieutenant).
March	Manfred ends the month with 74 victories; Lothar reaches 29.
April 7	Manfred is promoted to *Rittmeister* (cavalry captain).
April 9–17	German Lys Offensive.
April 20	Manfred scores victories 79 and 80.
April 21	Rittmeister Manfred Freiherr von Richthofen is shot down and killed over the Somme.

July 9	Oberleutnant Hermann Göring assumes command of Jadgeschwader 1.
November 11	Lothar ends the war with 40 victories.

1922

July 4	Lothar Freiherr von Richthofen is killed in a flying accident.

Books

Campbell, Christopher. *Aces and Aircraft of World War I*. New York: Greenwich House, 1984.

Cooper, Bryan, and John Batchelor. *Fighter: A History of Fighter Aircraft*. New York: Charles Scribner's Sons, 1973.

Dupuy, R. Ernest, and Trevor N. Dupuy. *The Encyclopedia of Military History: From 3500 B.C. to the Present*. Rev. ed. New York: Harper and Row, 1977.

Dupuy, Trevor N., Curt Johnson, and David L. Bongard. *The Harper Encyclopedia of Military Biography*. New York: HarperCollins, 1992.

Franks, Norman. *Aircraft Versus Aircraft: The Illustrated Story of Fighter Pilot Combat from 1914 to the Present Day*. London: Grub Street, 1998.

———. *Who Downed the Aces in WWI? Facts, Figures, and Photos on the Fate of Over 300 Top Pilots Flying Over the Western Front*. New York: Barnes & Noble, 1998.

Franks, Norman, and Alan Bennett. *The Red Baron's Last Flight: A Mystery Investigated*. London: Grub Street, 1997.

Franks, Norman, and Hal Giblin. *Under the Guns of the German Aces: Immelmann, Voss, Göring, Lothar von Richthofen: The Complete Record of Their Victories and Victims*. London: Grub Street, 1997.

Franks, Norman, Hal Giblin, and Nigel McCrery. *Under the Guns of the Red Baron: The Complete Record of Von Richthofen's Victories and Victims Fully Illustrated*. London: Grub Street, 1995.

Gibbons, Floyd. *The Red Knight of Germany*. War & Warriors Series. Costa Mesa, CA: Noontide Press, 1991.

Immelmann, Franz. *Immelmann: "The Eagle of Lille."* Vintage Aviation Library. Trans. Claud W. Sykes. Novato, CA: Presidio Press, 1990.

Jackson, Robert. *Fighter Pilots of World War I*. New York: St. Martin's Press, 1977.

Jane's Fighting Aircraft of World War I. Foreword by John W. R. Taylor. London: Studio Editions, 1990.

Kennett, Lee. *The First Air War, 1914–1918*. New York: Free Press, 1991.

Kilduff, Peter. *Richthofen: Beyond the Legend of the Red Baron*. New York: John Wiley & Sons, 1993.

Lawson, Eric and Jane. *The First Air Campaign: August 1914–November 1918*. Great Campaigns Series. Conshohocken, PA: Combined Books, 1996.

Longstreet, Stephen. *The Canvas Falcons: The Men and Planes of World War I.* New York: Barnes & Noble, 1995.

Longyard, William H. *Who's Who in Aviation History: 500 Biographies.* Novato, CA: Presidio Press, 1994.

Richthofen, Manfred von. *The Red Air Fighter.* Novato, CA: Presidio Press, 1990.

Treadwell, Terry C., and Alan C. Wood. *German Knights of the Air, 1914–1918: The Holders of the Orden Pour le Mérite.* New York: Barnes & Noble, 1997.

———. *The First Air War: A Pictorial History, 1914–1919.* New York: Barnes & Noble, 1996.

Tucker, Spencer C. *Who's Who in Twentieth-Century Warfare.* New York: Routledge, 2001.

———. *The European Powers in the First World War: An Encyclopedia.* New York: Garland Publishing, 1996.

Werner, Johannes. *Knight of Germany: Oswald Boelcke, German Ace.* Trans. Claud W. Sykes. Novato, CA: Presidio Press, 1985.

Wohl, Robert. *A Passion for Wings: Aviation and the Western Imagination 1908–1918.* New Haven: Yale University Press, 1994.

Periodicals

Carlson, John R. "The Rittmeister's Medals." Cross and Cockade Journal, Autumn 1964 (Vol. 5, No. 3), pp. 257–263.

Connell, Dennis. "The Richthofen Controversy; 1918–1962 (Part 2)." Cross and Cockade Journal, Summer 1967 (Vol. 8, No. 2), pp. 189–194.

Lcw, Christopher. "Bloody April." Over the Front, Fall 1998 (Vol. 13, No. 3), pp. 268–276.

McGuire, Frank R. "The Richthofen Controversy; 1918–1962 (Part 1)." Cross and Cockade Journal, Spring 1967 (Vol. 8, No. 1), pp. 43–51.

O'Dwyer, William J. "Post-Mortem: Richthofen." Cross and Cockade Journal, Winter 1969 (Vol. 10, No. 4), pp. 289–313.

Skelton, Marvin, compiler and editor. "The Use of Special Ammunition." Cross and Cockade Journal, Autumn 1982 (Vol. 23, No. 3), pp. 249–267.

Bishop, William A. *Winged Warfare: The Illustrated Classic Autobiography of Canadian World War I Ace Billy Bishop.* Toronto: McGraw-Hill Ryerson, 1990.

———. *Winged Peace: The Story of the Air Age.* Toronto: McGraw-Hill Ryerson, 1990.

Bowen, Ezra, and the editors of Time-Life Books. *Knights of the Air.* The Epic of Flight Series. Alexandria, VA: Time-Life Books, 1980.

Farwell, Byron. *Over There: The United States in the Great War, 1917–1918.* New York: W. W. Norton, 1999.

Gilbert, Martin. *The First World War: A Complete History.* New York: Henry Holt, 1999.

Keegan, John. *The First World War.* New York: Alfred A. Knopf, 1999.

Mason, Herbert Molloy, Jr. *Lafayette Escadrille.* New York: Konecky & Konecky, 1964.

Price, Alfred. *Sky Battles! Dramatic Air Warfare Actions.* London: Arms and Armour, 1993.

Rickenbacker, Edward V. *Fighting the Flying Circus.* Wings of War Series. Alexandria, VA: Time-Life Books, 1990.

Sims, Edward H. *The Aces Talk.* New York: Ballantine Books, 1972.

Strachan, Hew, ed. *World War I: A History.* New York: Oxford University Press, 1998.

Udet, Ernst. *Ace of the Iron Cross.* Air Combat Classics series. Stanley M.Ulanoff, ed.; trans. Richard K. Riehn. New York: Ace Books, 1970.

page:

Earle Rice Jr. is a former senior design engineer and technical writer in the aerospace industry. After serving nine years with the U.S. Marine Corps, he attended San Jose City College and Foothill College on the San Francisco Peninsula. He has devoted full time to his writing since 1993 and has written more than three dozen books for young adults. Earle is a member of the Society of Children's Book Writers and Illustrators; the League of World War I Aviation Historians and its UK-based sister organization, Cross & Cockade International, the United States Naval Institute, and the Air Force Association.